Live Passionately!

The Saving and Transforming Power of the Cross

by
Fr. Cedric Pisegna, C.P.

Live Passionately!

Forward 5
Live Passionately! 7
    Part I .... The Saving Power of the Cross
1 Astounding Work of Love 11
2 Pure and Living Faith 21
3 Reborn by Grace 31
4 Sharers of Salvation 41
5 All In the Passion 53
6 Union With God 77
    Part II The Transforming Power of the Cross
7 Crucified With Jesus 87
8 Humility Leads To Glory 91
9 Ocean of Love 107
10 Transformed In God 115
11 Trials Are Necessary 135
12 Walk the Walk 143
13 Memory of the Passion 149
14 Choose the Cross 157
15 Remain on the Cross 167
16 Shared Suffering 179
17 Love is a Fire 187
18 Joy in Progress 195
19 Purifying Fire 203
20 Clothed with Christ 217

  About the Author 221
  Inspirational Teachings by Fr Cedric 222
  The Congregation of the Passion 224

© 2000 Fr Cedric Pisegna
© 2011 Fifth Printing
All rights reserved

FOREWORD

"He was pierced for our offenses,
crushed for our sins;
upon him was the chastisement
that makes us whole,
by his stripes we were healed." (Isaiah 53:5)

I am grateful to all of you who have attended one of my missions and are reading this book. I appreciate all my generous benefactors and friends who support me by prayers, finances and friendship. I pray this book will be everything that God wants it to be for you.

I could not have completed this project without the partnership of Jim and Janice Carleton and Terry Matthews from Chico, California. Your work was such a grace to me. Thanks to Eileen Kelly of Beulah, Michigan for painting the beautiful butterfly on the cover for me. Thanks also to my Passionist Community for supporting me and encouraging me.

I dedicate this, my first book, to my Mom and Dad who always taught me to make my own choices and encouraged me in those decisions.

Jesus, your passion continues to make me stop, wonder and worship. Glory to you!

Good Friday, 2000

Fr. Cedric Pisegna, C.P.

Fr. Cedric Pisegna, C.P.

LIVE PASSIONATELY!

This is a book about living, living to the full. Jesus said, "I have come that you may have life and have it *abundantly.*" (John 10:10) This is his job description. This is why he came. It is this abundance that I'm interested in. I believe you are too.

Jesus was talking to people who were already alive when he made that statement. Since that is so, what he meant was he came to bring us something we don't already have. What did he mean? *Passionate living!* I always say, "Don't just live, live passionately!"

To live can mean simply to exist. Jesus came to bring us more than mere existence. His gifts were salvation, joy, and a new relationship with the living God. This is abundant living. We hunger for this deep within. We thirst for this in our hearts. Look within yourself now. Isn't there a craving for something more? Don't you have a deep desire to live more fully? That is why you are reading this book.

The dictionary defines passion as an intense emotion, a zeal or enthusiasm for life. It is zest and energy toward being the best you that you can be. It can be energy, such as sexual energy. Passion is also defined as the sufferings of Christ.

I am a Passionist priest. Sometimes people will pronounce the word incorrectly and call me a "passionate" priest. Well, yes, they are right. I am passionate too! When I professed my vows in 1985, I was determined to live with passion. My first vow is to remember, meditate upon and proclaim the Passion of Christ. His passion was his sufferings, but it was also the way he lived his life. Jesus was a man on fire with enthusiasm for God and said, "Yes" to God's will. He loved people. He celebrated life and lived extravagantly. His life was charged with significance and meaning. His attitude was positive and resilient. I don't know about you, but I want to respond to life like Jesus did!

Are you passionate? Are you on fire for Jesus? Do you have a good attitude toward your life and circumstances? Saint Irenaeus said, "The Glory of God is a person fully alive." I pray that this book will anoint you to discover and live the *abundant* life Jesus came to bring you. He died for you to have it. It is yours to possess! The devil doesn't want you to know about it. I invite you to ask the Holy Spirit to burn in your heart as you read this book. I pray that because of this book you won't just live; rather, you will *live passionately!*

† Part I †

The Saving Power of the Cross

1
ASTOUNDING WORK OF LOVE
"The passion is the greatest and most astounding work of divine love." (St. Paul of the Cross)

THE CROSS IS THE CRUX

I heard a story about one of my favorite preachers, Billy Graham. As the story goes, when he was a young preacher he was giving a revival in a small town. He had a letter in his hand that he wanted to mail. He saw a 10-year-old on the street and questioned him, "Young man, do you know the way to the post office?" "Sure," he replied. "Just go straight down the street and it is on your right." "Well thank you very much," Billy Graham said. "My name is Billy Graham and tonight I'll be at the First Baptist Church preaching about the way to get to heaven. I hope you can come!" "I don't think so mister," said the 10-year-old, scratching his head. "You don't even know the *way* to the post office!"

Jesus is "the Way, the Truth and the Life." (John 14:6) No one in the history of humanity has ever made such a claim. Jesus is the way that leads to God, the truth that melts away all confusion and the life that is abundant and eternal.

Many times I come to a town that I've never visited before to preach a mission. I'll drive in not knowing exactly where the church building is located. As I drive into town I will look up, and inevitably I will see a large cross on the steeple, usually the highest structure in town. That's how I locate the church. The cross points the way.

We are so very familiar with the cross, aren't we? We put it up on steeples, hang it around our necks, put it on our walls and I've even seen people wear it on their ears and tattoo it on their arms. It is the central symbol of all of Christianity and Catholicism. But what does it mean? What is its significance? Sometimes we can be so familiar with something that it loses power.

When I talk about the cross or crucifix, I am not talking about a piece of wood or metal you may have on your wall or around your neck. Rather I am talking about the historic event it symbolizes, the death and resurrection of Jesus of Nazareth some two thousand years ago. In and of itself, the religious object has no power; however, it can remind us and draw us into the reality of the Passion event.

WE PREACH CHRIST AND HIM CRUCIFIED
(1 Corinthians 1:23)

Paul Daneo (canonized St. Paul of the Cross–don't confuse him with St. John of the Cross) was a man of faith who lived in Italy in the 1700's. He sensed God calling him to raise up a congregation dedicated to the Passion, to the Cross of Jesus Christ. Many priests and lay people of his day had grown lackluster and lukewarm in their faith. Scores had lost the significance and meaning of the Cross of Jesus. Paul raised up a congregation whose purpose (and first vow) was to meditate on and proclaim the meaning of the Cross to all. Today Passionist religious are in over 50 countries of the world doing precisely this: contemplating and proclaiming the Cross of Jesus Christ in various ways. I praise God for my call to be a Passionist and proclaim Jesus. I have found such rich meaning in the Cross and as I meditate on it my understanding of it deepens. While I am growing in my grasp of its significance, there was a time in my life that I had no understanding of the Cross. Let me explain.

I was born and raised in a medium-sized town in western Massachusetts, Agawam. I was baptized Catholic as an infant and raised Catholic through my youth. My parents were very conscientious about getting me and my two older sisters brought up in our faith. While I didn't attend formal Catholic schools in those years, I did attend C.C.D. classes. We had our confirmation ceremony in the eighth grade. To be honest, I found Mass boring and most of what I was learning in religion class seemed powerless and irrelevant. I couldn't wait to finish, graduate from the eighth grade and get confirmed.

My two older sisters had already been confirmed and weren't going to church anymore. You see, my parents had the philosophy that after we "got through" the sacraments, we would be able to make our own decision about whether or not we would attend church. Confirmation, after all, was the sacrament of final initiation into the church. It was about becoming a mature Christian adult and being able to make decisions about faith matters for yourself. I knew once I was confirmed, then, like my sisters, I would be able to choose whether or not to go to church each Sunday. Of course, I wanted out. The sacrament that was supposed to be the great sacrament of final incorporation into the Church instead became for me the great sacrament of excommunication from the Church! After confirmation, I made my own decision not to attend Mass anymore. I would still go occasionally on Christmas and Easter when everybody went and my relatives were in town. After all, I had to make them think I went all the time!

To be truthful, for all intents and purposes, we were "cultural Catholics." We were raised in the faith in a big anonymous church where people went to Mass Sunday after Sunday and we hardly knew anyone sitting beside us. We were Catholic because that was the way we were raised, not because we chose it. It was part of our ethnic (Italian, Czech, and Albanian) heritage. I'm not saying we didn't pray and try. We did, but for the most part we had the externals of religion instead of a vital living relationship with God in Jesus. All during my teenage years I never attended a youth group, retreat, or mission. I never went to C.C.D. class and only attended Mass a few times a year.

PARTY TIME

Finally after my public high school days I went to college. The place where I eventually ended up going was a large secular state university: the University of Massachusetts at Amherst. UMass is a huge school of about 35,000 students. It is so large, in fact, there are dormitories everywhere. Five of those dorms are 22 stories high! I know because I lived on the 21st floor of one of them, John Adams. Can you imagine what went on in those dorms?

One Friday afternoon when I was a freshman, I was walking on campus toward one of those dorms. As I looked up, I couldn't miss an advertisement on the plate glass windows of the lounge on the 5th floor. It was unmistakable and unavoidable. Everyone could see it. Stuck to the windows of the lounge were posters. Each poster had a huge letter on it in different colors. Much to my delight I read the word P-A-R-T-Y! Now, when you are an 18-year-old and it's Friday night and you see a sign like that . . . what do you do? Go to the party of course!

I remember getting dressed up for the party. How do you get dressed up when you are 18 years old? I put on my best tight just-washed blue jeans. Then, I put on my fuzzy soft angora sweater. Now here is where this gets religious. Just before I went to college, Mom had given me a sterling silver cross with a sterling silver neck chain that glistened whenever the light hit it. I loved to wear that cross. It was kind of like my lucky charm. In fact, my faith at that time was so superstitious I felt if I was just wearing that cross nothing bad would happen to me.

As I stood there in front of the mirror, I put the cross on. As I examined myself, instead of putting it beneath my sweater, I wore it outside my sweater. You see, I was going to the party. I knew there would be some sweet young things at the party and I was hoping one of them would see the cross and think, "Well there's a fine, young, *Christian* guy, think I'll go talk to him!"

The party was as advertised–packed with people! Guys, girls, good music, lots to drink and it was crowded. My friend and I were standing there drinking some, uh, punch (ahem) and scoping out the room. As I scanned the room, I could hardly believe my eyes. There she was! She was 19 years old with long blonde hair and drop-dead gorgeous. As I looked, I couldn't help but notice she was looking at my cross from across the room. I thought to myself, "This thing is working like a charm! They write books about how to pick up girls. This ought to be on page ONE!"

Next thing I knew she began walking toward me. I remember thinking, "Stay calm Cedric, this will be a piece of cake, she is coming to you!" She walked right up to me, looked at the cross then looked me in the eyes.

I'll never forget what she said to me then. As she stared into my eyes with confidence she said, "Do you know what that cross means, or are you just wearing it to look good?" I was stunned. Here was this gorgeous young girl challenging me about the cross, and I was speechless. I didn't know what to say, because to be truthful, I was wearing the symbol of love, selflessness and sacrifice for my own self-aggrandizement so I could pick up a girl! I laugh about it now, but it wasn't funny at the time.

Well, I didn't get the girl, but I did get a dress–my religious habit! God works in strange and mysterious ways! The ways and extent God will go to woo a person to himself is interesting. Francis Thompson, an English mystic, has rightly called God the "Hound of Heaven." God will search for you, hunt for you, find you, and draw you to himself. God relentlessly pursues us. The challenge of that young girl is only one of the happenings that occurred in my life at that time. I remember watching Billy Graham on TV and seeing the joy those people seemed to have. "I want that," I thought. The play *Godspell* made me realize that something was lacking in my life. The movie *Jesus of Nazareth* showed me a beautiful Christ with integrity I had never known before. I began to become attracted and drawn to Jesus.

I don't know what your thoughts are about how God works. Psalm 139 says clearly it was God who knit you together in your mother's womb. You didn't just "happen." God intended for you to be before the world began. You are no mistake. God knows when we sit and when we stand. God knows every word on our lips even before we do. God surrounds us before and behind. In other words, whether you know it or not, God is *intimately* and *intricately involved* in our lives.

God will go to any extent to search you out and find you. God will use people, priests, books, the fine arts, plays, TV shows, movies, music, animals, creation, the Bible and anything else to call you to himself! Jesus would always say in his preaching, "You who have ears to hear, listen!" I pray you have the grace to truly open your eyes, listen with your ears, and perceive the multitude of ways God is using to draw you into a deep, personal relationship with him. Our God is an awesome God, glorious in majesty.

EVERYBODY'S GOT A HUNGRY HEART

For years I used to come into various parishes and preach about a song I heard that rang true in my life. It is by Bruce Springstein: "Everybody's Got a Hungry Heart." Time and time again in the song the chorus rings out: "Everybody's got a hungry heart, everybody's got a hungry heart, everybody's got a hungry heart . . ." That is so true. Deep inside us, in the core of our being, where we think, feel, decide, and what the Bible calls "our heart" is hungry. We have "heartache" for God. In fact, I believe the hunger and thirst for satisfaction is a sort of "homing device" the Lord places within us at birth so we will search for God. I believe you are reading this book because you are craving for God. That is a gift from God. You are following the blessing God placed in your heart when you were born. While you are searching for God, believe me, God is searching for you!

After the events of those days and I had just turned nineteen, I became aware of an intense hunger for something but I wasn't sure what. My heart was hungry. I'll never forget the days I would wake up in the morning, sit on the side of my bed, and wonder what all this was about. As I began to wipe the "sleepies" out of my eyes, I sensed a still small voice within me. It was the voice of my conscience. These are the words I heard as I looked around the bedroom: "What is this? I feel like I am missing something. I'm not happy. I am not satisfied. There is something more I don't yet have." Years ago St. Augustine wrote, "Our hearts were made for you, O Lord, and our hearts are restless until they rest in thee."

GOD'S WORD IS LIVING AND ACTIVE
(Hebrews 4:12)

I still remember the day I got fed up with feeling restless inside and decided to do something about it. I remembered my C.C.D. teachers had taught me that truth was supposed to be found in the Bible. I hungered for truth and wisdom. My parents had a huge family Bible on the bookshelf downstairs in their house. I thought to myself, "I'll look in the Bible for truth and find out for myself." There is a saying that curiosity killed the cat. Well, if you are curious enough and noble enough to search for yourself, it may just lead to life!

I sneaked downstairs one morning and saw the Bible on the shelf in the living room. As I grabbed for it, I first looked both ways to make sure no one saw me. I mean, if my parents ever saw me going for the Bible, that's worse than talking to them about sex! I took the Bible, blew the dust off the top of it and quietly made my way back to my room. Here I was, 19 years old, opening up the pages of the Bible on my own for the first time in my life. "Where do I begin?" I thought. I noticed that toward the end of the Bible there were lots of words in red. I understood those were the words of Jesus himself. I said to myself, "Forget the black and white, I'm going right for the red!"

As I sat on the edge of my bed and explored, something happened to me that I will never forget. I came to Matthew 7:7 where I saw lots of red. I read something that punched me right in the nose and made time stand still for a moment. "Ask, and it will be given to you; seek, and you will find; knock, and it will be opened to you." I had heard that before, but somehow there was a *now*ness to it. It was like it was just for me. Yes! Exactly what I was looking for. I came to discover years later when I studied this verse that in the Greek it really means, "**Keep on** asking, **keep on** seeking, **keep on** knocking" and you will find. It is not a one-time thing. Seeking is a process, day by day, minute by minute, constantly. Seeking is really a *lifelong* process. Most people ask or seek and if they don't receive right away, they grow discouraged and give up. There is no such thing as a microwave Christianity. Things take time. Conversion is a process.

As the days and weeks passed, I began asking. I remember praying for wisdom and truth. I wanted to know. I had a desire to learn. One of the books of the Bible that influenced my life at that time was the Book of Wisdom itself. Wisdom 6:17 says, "The beginning of Wisdom is the most sincere **desire** to learn." I had desire. I had hunger and thirst. This is the beginning of wisdom. You must be motivated to find and *not* give up. Be determined! God is the rewarder of all who seek him.

Seeking God, I found out, is not just about praying and reading the Bible. It is also about taking responsibility for your life. You cannot read the Bible without hearing the demands that it makes upon you. I loved "Ask and you shall receive" and I hated "Repent for the Kingdom is at hand." I knew I had to change, otherwise I would never receive all God had for me. Repentance simply means to change. Specifically, it means to turn away from whatever is sinful in one's life. That takes honesty and self-examination. This is another place where scores of people fall away. They aren't willing to look at themselves honestly and make the move they really need to make. Please understand–you must be motivated to turn from your sins to the living God or else there will be a major road block in the way of your receiving his love for you. It is this inner thrust that is the seed of living passionately.

2
PURE AND LIVING FAITH

"Every effort should be made to pray in pure and living faith, to seek God alone, to live in him, to languish with love for him . . ." (St. Paul of the Cross)

THROUGH FAITH AND FOR FAITH
(Romans 1:17)

Along with repentance, faith is needed. It takes some degree of faith to come to God in prayer or the Bible in the first place, but I have found that faith can grow. It increases as you read the Bible or spiritual books. It grows as you pray. Romans 10:17 clearly states, "Faith comes from what is heard, and what is heard comes by the preaching of Christ." In other words, whether you hear the word by reading it, by listening to a preacher on TV or in church, or by listening to good Christian music, faith comes when you "hear" the gospel message.

One of the goals I have at any of my missions is the *faith* of the people who come will increase and grow. Often there are a number of teenagers there. Many teenagers today do not understand the Gospel and have little faith in Jesus as savior. I know if they *hear* the Gospel proclaimed clearly, simply and enthusiastically, they will grow in faith. That faith can open them up to an experience of God. Billy Graham once said the Gospel has *built-in* power. In other words, if people can simply hear the good news proclaimed in an understandable way, they will experience something. Faith will come. Light will shine. People do change. There is power in the Gospel of Jesus Christ to change lives!

† Chapter 2 †

As I read the Bible as a young man, I kept seeing the word *believe*. It is everywhere in the Scriptures. It was as if that word became tattooed on my brain. Whenever I would want to give up or get discouraged about seeking God or feel faint in prayer, *believe* would well up within me. I pray as you read these words, you will know the *built-in* power of the Gospel. I believe God will grace you with faith and your reliance and trust in God will grow right now. It was faith that opened my heart up to an experience of God. Ephesians 2:8 says it well: "We are saved by grace, *through faith*." Even faith is a gift God wants you to have in full measure!

Once the Lord showed me the role faith plays in a person's life. It is a channel or conduit through which flows the invigorating life of God. I like to use the example of a fan I have in my room. It has a long electrical cord with a plug on the end of it. As long as it is unplugged, the fan is motionless. But once I plug it into the electrical outlet, the electricity flows *through the cord* and the fan begins to turn and oscillate. Faith is like that electrical cord. It is the channel through which salvation, grace, and the power of God flow. Once God's electricity flows in people, they move!

Once two eleven-year-olds were taking a shortcut through a cow pasture. As they walked through the field they turned and saw this huge bull with two large pointy, horns running toward them. They began to run as fast as they could but the bull was gaining on them. As they were running, one of the boys shouted to the other, "Quick! Do something! Pray!" The only prayer the other boy knew was table grace. He began, "Thank you Lord for what we are about to receive!"

I want to make one thing clear. A person doesn't "get" salvation, he or she "receives" it. There is a huge distinction here. Getting implies struggle and work. Receiving implies gift and ease. The Bible talks a lot about receiving. We *receive* forgiveness. We *receive* the Holy Spirit. We *receive* the love of God. We *receive* grace and mercy.

This terminology of receiving is also rightly present in sacramental theology. Notice, we don't *get* the Eucharist, we *receive* communion. No one gets forgiven, rather a person receives forgiveness. People will sometimes ask me, "Why do I have to go to confession? Can't I just pray to God on my own?" Well, yes you can pray to God on your own. However, most do not feel totally forgiven. Others do not truly forgive themselves. The sacrament of reconciliation, when celebrated well, helps a person to *receive* the forgiveness and touch of God. It also graces people to forgive themselves and to put their sin behind them.

I distribute communion to tens of thousands of different people each year. It is interesting to look at people's faces as they come and to watch their body language. Many still receive Christ's body on the tongue. Others open their hands in surrender as the host is placed on their palm. Still others (and I don't know where they learned this) will actually take or grab the host from me with their thumb and index finger as they come forward. I often wonder if that is symbolic of that person's trying to get Christ instead of surrendering and receiving him in faith.

I have a statement I love to share with people on my missions, "Believe and receive!" I pray that as you read this book, it will inspire your faith so you will be susceptible enough to receive all that Jesus died for to give you. "But to all who *received* him, who *believed* in his name, he gave power to become children of God . . ." (John 1:12)

FAITH IS COMPLETED BY WORKS
(James 2:22)

There is one other reality about faith I want to share with you. Faith or belief is not just some obscure, intangible welling up within the mind or heart of a person. The Gospel of John adds another perspective. If you page through the fourth Gospel you will see the word "believe" all over the place. It occurs 98 times. Robert Kysar, in his book *John the Maverick Gospel*, makes the point that John never uses the noun, faith or belief, but always and only the *verb*, to believe. I learned in elementary school that verbs are "action" words. In other words, for John, faith is always an active matter. Faith is something one does.

You must understand that faith is a continuing dynamic. On all my missions, I attempt to move people to make another quality decision for Christ (or for some, their first decision for Jesus). Faith is an over and over again decision for Jesus. Faith is persevering in prayer. Having faith is reaching out to the poor and needy. Faith is giving your witness to an unbeliever. Faith is turning away from your sin. Faith is forgiving and loving. Faith is a constant surrender. As I said above when I talked about the fan, it **moves!** This verse from James has always made total sense to me: "Show me your faith apart from your works, and I by my works will show you my faith." (James 2:18) Good works should flow from faith and complete faith. Faith and works are really two sides of one coin. You want to live passionately? Then **activate** your faith! The devil won't know what to do with you.

We have a TV antenna on the top of our roof at the monastery. Inside, there is a control to move the antenna north, south, east or west. If the antenna is facing in the wrong direction, the program looks all snowy. All I have to do is move the dial to turn the antenna toward the transmitter. Once that is done, the program will come in crystal clear.

Many Christians aren't receiving because they are facing in the wrong direction. What I mean by this is faith is like that antenna. Initially we get some reception, no matter how faint, by simply believing. Then, as we complete faith (Galatians 5:6, James 2:22) by repentance, obedience, prayer, and loving works, our antenna gets turned ever more correctly to the transmitter (God) and this fine tuning brings about clarity. Now technicians have come out with high definition TV. The images are sharp and very precise. When you come to Christ with the fullness of faith, you receive ever more sharply and clearly God's love for you personally. God is always transmitting his love to every person. The problem is many don't have their antennas up, never mind pointed in the right direction!

Prayer was difficult for me in those early days. Make no mistake about it, prayer takes faith, and flows from faith, especially when you are going through trials and tribulations. I was so tempted to doubt that God was hearing me at times. It would seem like my words were just bouncing off the walls and were having no effect. It seemed like I wasn't getting any results. But I was persistent and continued to believe and press on in my prayer life.

It's amazing the temptations that come to a person who is trying to grow spiritually. I can remember my friends coming to my door or calling me saying, "C'mon out and party, it's Friday night!" It was hard to resist, but if you want to live passionately, you have to be determined to spend time in prayer and spiritual reading. I told them, "No thanks, I want to spend time on my own."

GOD IS LOVE
(1 John 4:16)

After months and months of praying, repenting, reading, believing, growing, being determined, reading, growing, praying, believing, and repenting, I started to change. My heart began to open to the unconditional love of God. I want to make one thing perfectly clear right now. God loves you just the way you are. God will never love you any more than he does right now. That is simply the way God is. However, our ability to **receive** God's love changes as we change and open ourselves up to God. Why the necessity of repentance, obedience, believing, praying, celebrating the sacraments, and studying the Bible? Because these are all means for us to discover, absorb, and know the love God has for us. These actions make us susceptible to being touched by God.

Please understand that we don't do things to try to get God to love us more. Rather we do things in faith to seek the God of love and open our hearts to that love. I have found that it is not because I parade around the country preaching Jesus to thousands of people that God loves me. Rather, I parade around the country *because* God loves me. My priesthood is one of thanksgiving. Psalm 116:13 says, "How shall I give thanks to the Lord? The cup of salvation I will raise!" When I am presiding at Mass and I lift up the cup with the blood of Christ, I often think of this. Give thanks to the Lord because he is good and his mercy endures forever. A major part of living passionately is "thanks-living." It is a life-style of giving thanks. It is a continuous attitude of gratitude. God is so worthy to be praised.

I heard a story about a grandmother who had a granddaughter and grandson for whom she was buying Christmas presents. She had already bought a number of presents for them and just needed one small present more for each. While in a mall she saw a poster store and thought to herself, "Perfect." As she searched through the selections of posters she saw one with a young man on a surf board riding a wave. Since her grandson loved surfing she wrote down the number of the poster and kept flipping looking for one for her granddaughter. She came upon a poster of a mountain scene with flashy yellow meadow flowers. She wrote down the number of that poster and gave the numbers to the clerk. Having received the rolled up posters, she wrapped them in Christmas paper and put them under the tree.

When Christmas day came the grandson opened his poster and unfurled it to find a stunning surf scene. "Thank you, Grandma, I love it!" he said. "I'll put it on my bedroom wall." Then it was the granddaughter's turn. When she opened her poster her mouth dropped open in surprise. Everyone wondered what she was seeing. Then she turned the poster around and there was a big pink hippopotamus. Underneath was the caption, "But I love you ***just the way you are!***" Everyone chuckled and the grandmother said the clerk must have made a mistake and she would gladly take it back. "That's OK, Grandma," the teenage girl said, "I'll keep it."

A month later the grandmother got a letter in the mail from her granddaughter. "Grandma," she wrote,

"I just wanted you to know how much your poster gift has meant to me. Lately I have been feeling really ugly and bad about myself. I just had a breakup with my boyfriend. At times I come home from school, flop myself on my bed, and look up at that poster. I see the pink hippopotamus and read the caption: 'But I love you just the way you are!' I can't tell you what strength that has given me in the midst of my insecurities. Thank you, Grandma."

The basic message and truth about Catholicism and Christianity itself is that God loves us just the way we are. We can't earn it. We don't deserve it. We can never merit it. God's love is without boundaries, passionate and unparalleled. God's love is generous, forgiving, saving, tender, gentle, and intimate. The word in the Greek for this is *agape*. The word refers to the way God loves. It is the type of love that gives generously *without expecting anything in return*. In other words, there are no strings attached. Proclaiming this deep, passionate love of God is really the motivation behind every mission I preach. My goal is that through music, prayer, and preaching an atmosphere will be created such that people will become susceptible and open enough to experience God's love afresh.

This is wonderful news! Spend some time thinking and meditating on this truth. Right now, just as you are, you are loved. Maybe you don't feel good about yourself. Possibly you are a parent whose children have fallen away from the faith. Perhaps you have failed in some business venture and are lacking funds. It could be that you have low self-esteem and hate the way you look. You are insecure because of this. Well, Jesus is the cure for the insecure! Perhaps you just feel like a big, old, pink hippopotamus. The truth is no matter how you look, feel, or perform, God is in love with you just the way you are.

While that is true, he loves us too much to *leave us that way*. We are "on the way" and God is constantly changing us to be like Christ.

3
REBORN BY GRACE

"Every time your spirit is centered in God . . . it is certain your soul is being reborn in the Divine Word to a new life of grace and love." (St. Paul of the Cross)

AMAZING GRACE

Recently I read a newspaper article that caught my eye. Catholics and Lutherans finally reached agreement about salvation. A disagreement over how to achieve salvation was the core issue that led Martin Luther to split the western Christian church with the reformation. Simply put, Protestants have believed that salvation comes through faith alone, while Catholics have taught that it is a combination of faith and good works that saves. Listen to this recent statement from the "Joint Declaration on Justification (salvation) by Faith." "Together we confess: by **grace alone**, in faith in Christ's saving work and not because of any merit on our part, we are accepted by God and receive the Holy Spirit, who renews our hearts while equipping and calling us to good works." It is not by faith *and* our good works that we are saved. Our Church teaches that we are saved by faith in Jesus and that this faith spurs us on to do good works. We are not saved by our works or by our own goodness. The point here is that salvation comes from the free unconditional love of God and is not dependent on our goodness.

IT IS THE GIFT OF GOD
(Ephesians 2:8)

I'd like to illustrate what I mean about grace by continuing my own story. After months and months of opening myself up to God through believing, prayer and repentance, I had an experience one night. Some have intense experiences of God and others don't. Why this happens is a mystery to me. I am telling you about my experience here not to make you think you have to be like Fr. Cedric, but rather, so that you will continue to open yourself up to whatever God may have in store for you.

I will never forget that hot July night in 1977. I'm not even sure I had prayed before hopping into bed. But as I lay there and began to drift off to sleep, I suddenly received a visitation from God. I was overwhelmed and saturated with light, glory, and peace. I experienced God's glory. God's glory is his rhythmic energy that flows as pleasure through a person's spirit. It is electricity and power. I was taught that it will be God's glorious presence that will raise us up from the dead. I lost all track of time and space. I was enveloped by love.

I have been loved by my mom and dad. I have been loved by friends, relatives, and girl friends. But I had *never* experienced love like that before. God's love is deep, powerful, eternal, and blissful. God's love is intense and overwhelming! We Passionists pray the Psalms in our chapel at morning prayer. One of my favorite Psalms that I love to chant is Psalm 118: "The steadfast love of the Lord endures forever!" It is God's love that upholds the universe. It was God's love that had you in mind before you were created. What God revealed to me at that moment is that not only did he love me, but God was **in love** with me (and you too!). What that means is that there is a deep longing in God's heart for relationship and intimacy and his love craves union. You are the beloved of God!

After some time I came to myself again and found myself sobbing and crying. As I went to my sink to wash up, I realized that when a baby is born it cries. I realized that I had just been reborn.

People experience change in varied ways: gradually over time, suddenly, or a combination of both. Both experiences are good and valid. Both are from God. God is mysterious and works in various people's lives in a multitude of ways. Our part is to be trusting, open, and vulnerable. God will do his part. Change in our lives is a process. Part of that process is the "suddenlies." At any time, anywhere, in any way, God can show up and touch you powerfully. Suddenly. However most of the time, we change little by little, step by step, gradually. Please be hopeful for significant moments, however. The Bible is full of them!

As I continued to read the Scriptures and reflect on my having been touched and my continuing experience of the Holy Spirit, I put two and two together. I began to have a profound *inner knowing* that I was **saved**. The Holy Spirit was confirming in me what I was reading in the Bible. One of the major truths that I proclaim on my mission campaigns, (my *mission* so to speak) is that we can **know** salvation in the Catholic Church. Are you saved?

BLESSED ASSURANCE

You might be thinking, "Well Fr. Cedric, I was taught that thinking you are saved is the sin of presumption." Actually, if you read the new *Catechism of the Catholic Church,* you will see that presumption is actually a sin against hope. In paragraph #2092 we read: "There are two kinds of presumption. Either man presumes upon his own capacities, (hoping to save himself without help from on high), or he presumes upon God's almighty power or his mercy (hoping to obtain his forgiveness without conversion and glory without merit)." In other words, far from sinning by thinking you are saved, presumption is the sin of thinking you can *save yourself* by your *own good works*! While some think knowing you are saved is presumption, I like to think of it as "blessed assurance." That's exactly what faith in God's love brings: assurance.

Hebrews 11:1 states: "Now faith is the *assurance* of things hoped for." When you look up assurance in the dictionary you find definitions such as confidence, freedom, from doubt, certainty, and boldness. These are the qualities the early apostles had! But even more than confidence, there is an "inner knowing" that comes from the Holy Spirit. This is one of my favorite verses in the Bible: "It is the (Holy) Spirit himself *bearing witness* with our spirit that we *are* children of God . . ." (Romans 8:16). I always love the reading on All Saint's Day (November 1) when we hear, "Beloved we are God's children *now.*" (1 John 3:2) One of the major goals of this book is that you will trust in Jesus for salvation. That through believing you are saved, you will have righteousness, peace, and joy. That's living passionately!

There is no greater joy than knowing you are saved. Nehemiah 8:10 says, "The joy of the *Lord* is your strength." Salvation brings an inner, transcendent joy that cannot be taken away from you. This joy is yours to revel in no matter the circumstance. This joy actually strengthens you to deal with the difficulties of life. It is amazing to me how many people are living in confusion or trying to be strong by themselves. The saved are not like this. You have joy to draw upon. The joy of knowing you belong to God and that God will protect you forever is your strength. The joy of knowing you are a citizen of heaven will help you whatever the storm or trial. (See Philippians 3:20)

Knowing salvation is absolutely **foundational** to knowing the abundant life that Jesus offers. How are you going to experience real joy without knowing that you are saved? How will you ever know peace without knowing what God has done for you? How will you ever feel right about yourself unless you know that you are righteous through Christ? The reason John wrote his three letters is so you may **know that you have eternal life!** (1 John 5:13)

FIRM FOUNDATIONS

My dad taught me a lot about foundations. Dad was a carpenter and I used to work with him while I was in college. Often we would lay the foundations for the buildings we were constructing. First, we would survey the land with a surveying scope, plumb bobs, and all kinds of measuring tools. Before any concrete for the foundation was poured, we would spend hours getting the forms in proper place to receive the concrete. I used to get frustrated at the length of time it took to get everything just right. My stomach would be growling and I'd be looking at my watch wondering when we were finally going to lunch. Sometimes we'd check the same corner over and over again until it was perfect. Dad taught me that it was very important to be meticulous with laying the foundation. If any of it was out of whack ,the rest of the project would be askew. It was crucial to have everything precise to begin with so everything else would be built on a solid, level, firm foundation.

"For we who have *believed* enter into that rest . . ." (Hebrews 4:3) Hebrews chapters 3 and 4 talk about the "rest" of God. This a place of peace, calm and joy that comes from knowing you are saved. It comes only through faith and trust. It is received through confidence and trust in the living God. If you are looking for rest and the peace which is a major component of living passionately, you must believe in the salvation God has for you in Christ. It is absolutely foundational to living the abundant life. Otherwise there will always be fear, doubt, confusion, and separation from God.

DECISION TIME

When I began preaching missions, I used to have one night dedicated to "altar calls." If you are not familiar with this, an altar call is a moment when a person can choose to come forward and give or rededicate his or her life to Christ. It is done in the open in front of everyone and means that you must publicly get out of your chair. Many think this is a Protestant-type service, but in reality, we do this in the Catholic Church all the time. For example, at Mass, we get up and come forward to receive Christ in communion. On Good Friday, we get up and come forward and venerate the cross. On Ash Wednesday, we publicly come forward and get ashes on our foreheads. The symbol of our faith and salvation is there for all to see.

An altar call during a mission is a special time of grace. It is a moment of inspiration when a person can make a **quality** decision for Jesus Christ. I was taught in moral theology that people have within them a fundamental stance and a fundamental option. The fundamental stance is the basic thrust of their life and where they are heading. Most decisions made flow from this direction and also patterned decisions **determine** this direction. The fundamental option is the decisions we make that should flow with the direction and goal we have in mind (our fundamental stance).

Sometimes we decide to do things that depart from our fundamental stance or thrust of our life. We sin. We backslide. We make bad choices. We lose our way. Our stance in life becomes clouded and confused. As a country western singer once sang, "If you don't stand for something, you'll fall for anything!" An altar call can reorient a person's fundamental option toward Jesus. A radical call to Christ and a public move symbolizes what is going on in the person's heart. A new choice for Jesus (fundamental option) can solidify and strengthen and even change the fundamental stance of a person.

ADAM, WHERE ARE YOU?
(Genesis 3:9)

One day the absentminded G.K. Chesterton was taking a train ride. After the train got moving, the conductor came over to him and said, "Sir, do you have your ticket?" At this, G.K. began to feel around in all his pockets searching for his train ticket. Exasperated, he replied, "I can't find my ticket!" "That's OK, Mr. Chesterton, I know that you are a man of integrity, no problem," replied the conductor. "No, wait!" said G.K., "I have to find my ticket. I don't know where I am going!"

Many people feel like they are on a train ride and are not sure where they are going morally. Some feel like they are on a fast-moving river and they "go with the flow." Christians are those who make conscious decisions over and over, every day, for Christ. We should always be evaluating our choices and decisions and making sure they follow the demands of Christ. One of the hardest sayings in the Gospel is "Enter by the *narrow* gate; for the gate is wide and the way is easy, that leads to destruction, and those who enter by it are many. For the gate is narrow and the way is hard, that leads to life, and those who find it are few." (Matthew 7:13-14) A mission is a time to make a stand for Christ and reorient your choices toward that stance. You can succumb to the temptations of evil or surrender to the one who leads you to life.

I usually got a tremendous response when I offered the altar call. At first, a few people would stream forward, then others, when they saw they wouldn't be alone if they made a move, jumped up also. I found this style of ministering radical yet effective. Recently, I've put the emphasis on the call to come to confession. Certainly, our sacrament of reconciliation is an altar call type of service. In addition to confession on all of my missions, I have the people kneel and pray a prayer of self-surrender.

I am praying that this book will have an impact on you much like a mission would. It provides a "place" whereby God can touch you and help you reorient yourself and your choices toward Christ. I am inviting you at this moment to make a move with God. I am hoping this book will help you take a new stance for Jesus. I invite you right now, at this very moment, to surrender your doubts, lack of faith or trust, and confusion about salvation to the Lord. Simply give yourself to God right *now*, right where you are. You might want to pray something like this:

Prayer of Self-Surrender to Jesus

Jesus, I come to you in faith.
Just as I am.
I believe you died to save me.
I want that blessed assurance.
Please come into my heart in a new way.
Touch me, renew me, and inspire my faith.
I surrender the person I am to you.
Take me, Lord, and change me.
I love you Jesus.
AMEN!

I am praying for you as I write this book that the Holy Spirit will do a beautiful work in you. I pray that you will be freed from feeling that God is out to condemn you. I pray that you will be delivered from fears, especially the fear of death. (Hebrews 2:15) I believe that you will also be loosed from the tyranny of feeling like you have to "earn" it and be good enough to be able to go to heaven. If there was anyone who could have claimed her good works as a means of salvation, it was Mother Teresa. Even Mother Teresa, called a living saint while she was with us, said she was going to heaven not because of her good works, but because of what Jesus did for her.

I believe you will know that you are *right* with God through Jesus. Because of this, you will experience deep moments of peace. The joy of the Lord will be your strength. This is your heritage as a child of God—not condemnation, fear, and doubt. You will know in your heart the glorious truth that the kingdom of God is righteousness, peace, and joy in the Holy Spirit! (Romans 14:17)

4
SHARERS OF SALVATION
"The Church was founded to spread the Kingdom of God, to make everyone sharers in redemption and salvation . . ."
(Passionist Constitutions #62)

TODAY SALVATION HAS COME TO THIS HOUSE
(Luke 19:9)

I remember my preaching teacher in theology school rightly taught us not to throw theological words out at people. People won't understand what you mean. Words like salvation, righteousness, justification, redemption, and expiation are dangerous words. They are dangerous for preachers because if you use them too much or too often, you can put people to sleep! Many people stop listening unless you explore the word and explain it in everyday language.

I'd like to break open the reality of salvation by using some contemporary, easily understandable examples. I am typing this book on my laptop computer. Someone gave this to me as a gift. I often take it with me as I travel. I edit my website on it, write letters, and send faxes. I have noticed that a lot of computer language has religious terminology in it. For example, whenever I write a letter and am about to close the document and exit the computer, the computer is programmed to ask me a question. The question that it asks me before I exit is: "Do you want to save the document? Yes or No." If I click on Yes, the document is *preserved, held on to* and *kept* exactly the way I typed it in. Even pictures, images and graphics are preserved just the way they were imported.

† Chapter 4 †

I WANNA HOLD YOUR HAND
(Isaiah 42:6)

The next time I come to the computer and call up the document, it is opened **exactly** the way it was typed in. Every comma, period, letter, and sentence is preserved precisely as it was created. Do you understand that God loves you so much that *you* will be preserved, kept, and held onto forever? I love what Jesus said in John 10:28, "I give them (my sheep) eternal life and they shall never perish, and *no one shall snatch them out of my hand*." As many artists have sung: "Put your hand in the hands of the man who stilled the water!" No one can snatch us out of his mighty hands.

Do you know that that which makes you *you*; your person, your heart, your innermost being, *will be held on to?* Mysteriously, we will be changed, but we will still be conscious of being who we are. We will be aware of our existence and able to know that we have eternal life. What joy will flood our hearts! God is so passionately in love with us that he wants us to live forever! Sometimes when I preach this on missions I actually jump in the air! If you can't get excited about this, then what can you get excited about?

I am a missionary priest. I come to proclaim Good News. This is my vocation and the essence of my call. It is eternal life that excites me and colors my life here on earth. The assurance of heaven thrills me with hope, flavors me with joy, and graces me with rest and peace. If you want to live passionately, then experiencing salvation (knowing eternal life) is crucial and foundational. Otherwise you will always have doubts and uncertainty. I say this boldly and clearly: Jesus came to save you and gift you with eternal life! If our Church offers us anything, it is salvation! This is the main purpose of the Church on earth.

YOU WERE SEALED WITH THE SPIRIT
(Ephesians 1:13)

You'll notice that I am equating salvation with being preserved forever and with eternal life. But there is more. While eternal life gives us hope to inspire our days now, salvation is also the presence of God protecting us each day. Many are very zealous about coming to the missions I preach and love to sit right up front. Sometimes because of the crowds, they will place a book on the spot where their friend or relative will be sitting because they are out parking the car or going to the rest room. If someone tries to sit in that spot, they see the book and the person sitting there says, "Sorry, this seat is **saved**." In other words, you'd better not sit there, this place is taken, it is protected, it is MY seat.

Similarly, when you are saved, God's favor, blessing, and protection is on your life! This is a glorious truth. I love Psalm 125:2: "As the mountains surround Jerusalem, so the Lord surrounds his people from this time forth forevermore." When I listen to "surround sound" stereos, the music is full and rich and seems to be coming at you from all directions. God is surrounding you right now. His hand is upon you. When evil tries to get to you and harm your life, God says, "Sorry, this person is saved. Better not touch him or her. He is taken and protected. She is mine." There are many verses in the Bible that attest to this.

For example, when we are "sealed" with the Holy Spirit at confirmation, God has stamped his seal of **ownership** upon us. Notice how the writer of Ephesians connects being sealed with the Spirit with salvation in Ephesians 1:13. Some time back we had our long driveway at Christ the King Retreat Center in Sacramento "sealed." Workmen came and applied a sealant to make it look newer and to protect it from cracking. Age, the hot sun, and a constant flow of traffic make the tar crack. The Lord told me once that the purpose of the Holy Spirit's "sealing" is to renew us and to keep us from "cracking up" when the traffic and storms hit us!

DIVINE CONNECTIONS

As I travel the country, I meet a lot of people. I counsel scores in the confessional. I meet many on airplanes. I talk with people openly and casually. Because I am a priest, I hear a lot of different "religious" things from people. Every once in a while I meet a person who has had an encounter with a being they term to be an angel. I have heard unexplainable stories from people who believe that God sent an angel to them to warn them or protect them. My faith is encouraged as I hear these sincere stories. Our Church has always believed in angels. On October 2, for example, we liturgically celebrate the presence and activity of our guardian angels. What a grace to know that God is so involved in our lives that he mysteriously has appointed an angel to guard us!

I typically try to appreciate in prayer the ways God has protected me. For example, when I drive or fly somewhere, I will pray for protection and thank God when I arrive safely. Sometimes I will meet a harsh, mean-spirited person out in the world and thank God that I don't have that person as my boss or have to deal with that person day after day. I praise God for the health I enjoy and know it could be otherwise. I worship God for delivering me from earthquakes, floods, fires, tornadoes and hurricanes. Instead of taking it for granted that I've never been in a natural disaster, I appreciate it as a miracle from God. Sometimes you have to thank God for the things that *haven't* happened to you, as well as praise God for the good things you do have! This is God's protection and providence in your life, and it takes a person of faith, one who is saved, to appreciate God's activity.

Amy Grant is one of my favorite Christian artists. She produced an award-winning song in 1984 simply called "Angels." In this song, she reminds us of how God's angels are traveling with us wherever we go and whatever we do in our lives.

My mother is especially attracted to angels. Whenever I visit her house, I see little statues of them everywhere. One portrait is especially intriguing. My Mom and Dad used to create stained-glass window figures. Above their fireplace mantle hangs their best piece. It is a tall, young angel with flowing, luminous hair. His eyes mean business, yet there is gentleness about him. My parents designed the stained-glass window with a light behind it that can be turned on and off. The colors come to life when the light is on allowing the majesty and beauty of the angel to be seen. Angels aren't "little fat cherubs" resembling those on Hallmark cards. They are beautiful, powerful warriors. They are also tender messengers that bring good news as Gabriel brought to Mary.

What must these messengers of God be like? We are told they are "ministering spirits" sent to help those who will inherit salvation. (Heb. 1:14) Billy Graham wrote an eye-opening book called Angels. In this book, he documents many of the Scriptures about angels and tells of their purpose. Our Catholic Catechism tells us they are intelligent, immortal, and have wonderful glory (#330) How wonderful it is to know that God helps us and guards us through these wonderful beings of light. We may not see it or know it altogether, but they are there. When is the last time you prayed to your guardian angel? God comes to help us in many ways. Certainly one of these ways is by his countless angels.

Every morning we Passionists begin our Liturgy of the Hours asking for God's help. We begin by expressing the words of Psalm 38:22: "God come to my assistance. O Lord make haste to help me!" What a joy it is to know the help, protection, and aid of God in every circumstance.

KNOCKING AT HEAVEN'S DOOR

There is another sense of being saved that I want to share with you. I grew up in Massachusetts and loved to play sports. I was good at baseball, golf, tennis, and soccer. I played soccer on my high school team and because I was tall and agile, I became a goalie.

Every once in a while the forwards from the other team would advance, dribble around our fullbacks, and be heading toward the goal. Then, I would be the only thing that stood between them and a score. I can remember the time a forward shot the ball at the net and I dove and grabbed it in midair, stopping it from going into the goal. I heard someone shout, "SAVE!" I saved the ball *from* going into the net *for* our team. Pardon my bluntness here, but when we are saved, God saves us *from* hell *for* heaven. That is God's goal for your life.

When God saves us, we are delivered from an eternity of separation from his love. As I said before, God wants us to live forever with him. Make no mistake about it. As a missionary and as a pastor of your soul, I want to make it clear to you that there is a heaven and there is a hell and that Jesus suffered an intolerable torturous death to save us **from death for heaven**. Many people today are looking for a teacher or guru or wise man to guide their lives. What we *truly need* more than anything else (and God knew this) is a *savior*. In fact, remember what the angel said to Joseph when he appeared to him, "You shall call his name Jesus for he will save his people from their sins (and their consequences)." (Matthew 1:21) The very name Jesus means savior. That is his name and salvation was his mission.

First of all, Jesus came to deliver us from hell. Hell is separation from God as well as a place of shame and regret. Those of you who have lost a close loved one to death know the pain of separation. Before I entered the seminary, I had a number of relationships with women. I learned a lot about life and about myself through these relationships. At some point, every one of those relationships ended. I can still remember the intense pain of being "hurt" by the separation. The pain was so great that sometimes there were physical symptoms such as nausea and headaches. One of the worst realities in life is being separated from the one you are in love with. Loneliness, desolation, and despair can ensue.

Imagine the pain, the shame, and the regret of being separated forever from the one who gave us our being and everything we ever had and offered us his love every day. Because of lack of appreciation and selfishness, many neglect, deny, and spurn that love. People are willfully turning away. One day they will get just what they chose on earth: separation from God. God will never force himself on anyone. God allows us to choose.

I was sitting outside praying one day when God revealed this to me: those who trust in God and love him will *never be separated from him*. I was thinking about the uncertainty of death and how that would seemingly separate us from God. Then I was given this thought: my prior nonexistence (before I was born) wasn't able to separate me from God. Even when I was not, God willed me into being. Not even my nothingness and nonexistence could separate me from God!! If God could create me out of nothingness, then I am convinced that not even death will separate us. A person who has died is easy for God. They already were. God can raise them up again. The hard part, it seems to me, was creating our being out of **nothing**! If, when you were *nothing*, God called you into being, how much more now that you are, will God be able to bring you back to life again! This is a marvelous truth. Our God is ABLE!

I love Romans chapter 8. It is my favorite chapter in all of the Bible. It climaxes with these stunning words of St. Paul:

> If God is for us, who can be against us? God who did not spare his own Son but gave him up for us all, will he not also give us all things with him? Who shall separate us from the love of Christ? Shall tribulation, or distress, or persecution, or famine, or nakedness, or peril, or sword? No, in all these things we are more than

conquerors through him who loved us. For I am sure that neither death, nor life, nor angels, nor principalities, nor things present, nor things to come, nor powers, nor height, nor depth, nor anything else in all creation, will be able to separate us from the love of God in Christ Jesus our Lord. (Romans 8:31,32,35,37-39)

The good news is that by our faith in God's love, not even death will separate us from God. We are saved from death and separation from God for eternal union with God. God has a definite plan and goal for us: heaven!

BEHOLD, I MAKE ALL THINGS NEW
(Revelation 21:5)

Heaven will be a place of complete peace and rest from our labors. Everything we have ever desired will be there for us to enjoy. We will have new glorified bodies that will never grow old or wear out. Think of it: a reality where there will be no more dying, lying, sighing or crying. We will be reunited with our loved ones. The sound of song and rejoicing will be heard there!

But there will be one small problem: there will be a high unemployment rate in heaven. That's right. There will be no need for doctors, lawyers, politicians, and funeral directors. Policemen, firemen, and locksmiths will all be out of work! However if you are interested in a job, please give me a call because I'll need a grounds keeper for my signature 36 hole golf course behind my mansion!

Speaking of golf, I heard the story of an avid golfer who fell asleep and had a dream. An angel appeared to him in the dream and said, "I've got some good news, and sorry, some bad news." The man said, "Great! What's the good news?" "The good news," the angel replied, "is that there are golf courses in Heaven and they are beautiful beyond compare!" "So, then, what's the bad news?" the man queried. "The bad news is, you have a tee time at 9 tomorrow morning!"

Please understand that heaven is real and will be full of delights. I remember soon after I gave my heart to Jesus when I was nineteen, God gave me a revelation about heaven. It was so beautiful and gracious that it has colored my life and preaching ever since. There was once a movie called *The Land That Time Forgot*. I have come to understand that because of the noise, stress, idols, and cares of this world, we have "forgotten" heaven deep in our spirit. We need revelation in order to grasp it. I invite you to ask for revelation and wisdom about heaven. Your heavenly Father may just allow you to "remember" the thrilling beauty of heaven. We have a glorious future!

As much as I try to enjoy my life on earth, I know that my heart was made for more. There is such an incompleteness here. It is good to be in touch with this longing and hunger for completeness. We will never be fully happy and satisfied in this life. You were made for heaven and heaven was made for you. On that day, we will worship God face to face and be caught up in God's glory. God will himself wipe away every tear from our eyes. Heaven is our true home: we are but pilgrims on the journey home. "In this hope (of heaven) we are saved." (Romans 8:24) Jesus went to prepare a place for us and the Holy Spirit is preparing us for the place!

I heard a story about three women who were discussing what they would be buried with when they die. The first one said, "When I die, I want to be buried wearing the diamond ring my husband gave me." The second one said, "I have a pearl necklace that has been handed down to me from my great-grandmother. I want to be buried with it." The third one thought for a moment and replied, "I want to be buried with a fork." "A fork!" the women replied. "Why would you possibly want to be buried with a fork?" "Because when I was a little girl, whenever we would finish our dinner my mother would always tell us to keep our fork for dessert. I want everyone who sees that fork in the casket with me to know that the *best is yet to come*!"

NOBLE VESSELS
(2 Timothy 2:20)

One other contemporary example will help break open the notion of what it means to be saved. I like to do the grocery shopping for our community in Sacramento. When I go to the store, I look for items that have a sign below them saying, "Club Savings." I signed up for a club card at no cost. At the end of my shopping, I go to the register and they total up what I bought. Then I slide the club card in the register and suddenly, the final total is reduced considerably. All the items that were "on sale" are taken off the total. For example, if my total originally was $75. The reduced total is $50 after I slide my club card. Then the printed receipt emerges and states, "Thank you for shopping with us, you *saved* $25 today!"

That $25 is money now in my pocket that I can use for something else. There is an "alternate use" for the money. The money which would have been spent on groceries can now be used for paying other bills. Who are you being used for? Are you being used for your own pursuits, the devil, or God? It is clear to me that before I came to

Jesus I was living my life for myself. I didn't do much to help people and was pretty independent. Evil had a grip on me as I worshiped the things of this world and sought false pleasures. I was a slave to sin.

But now that I have surrendered myself to Jesus, I am being used for something else. God is using me for his own purposes. He has found an "alternative use" for my life. I have become a person who prays, worships, gives, serves, loves, and is concerned about God's kingdom *first*. That is the hallmark of one who is saved.

Are you living for yourself or for God? When you are saved, God will make use of you. You will live the will of God for your life. Listen to these beautiful verses from St. Paul: "I appeal to you therefore, brothers and sisters, by the mercies of God to present your very selves as a living sacrifice, holy and acceptable to God, which is your spiritual worship. Do not be conformed to this world but be transformed . . ." (Romans 12:1,2)

When they focus on salvation or the idea of eternal life many people think only of eternity and the "sweet by and by." That is so far from the truth of salvation that Jesus came to bring. As I said above, to be saved means that you will be preserved for heaven. However, if you have been reading between the lines, you will see that salvation and eternal life are *present realities* that color and flavor our lives *now*. Putting it another way, salvation is a new quality of life now that empowers you to live passionately. It is a life filled with hope rather than despair. It is a life of protection and favor from God rather than walking in darkness. It is a full life of being used by God to have an impact on others' lives. Salvation is for *here* as well as hereafter.

5
ALL IN THE PASSION
"All is to be found in the Passion of Jesus."
(St. Paul of the Cross)

CHRIST CRUCIFIED IS THE POWER AND WISDOM OF GOD (1 CORINTHIANS 1:24)

Every time I come to another church to preach a mission, I am fascinated with the architecture of the various buildings. I preach in old churches, new churches, long and short buildings, wide and narrow edifices. Some spaces have pillars; others are wide open. The stained glass windows can be stunning. Tabernacles containing the Blessed Sacrament are in various locations. I love to try to find them. I am particularly interested in the sanctuary and sound systems for preaching purposes.

Usually, during the course of the week that I am in a particular place, I will go into the church building by myself and explore. It's fun for me to find all the various places in the church where the cross is displayed. I've seen crosses in the sanctuaries, on the altar, etched in stained glass, on the walls (stations), carved into pews and pulpits, and on the lights above. There is usually a prominent display of a crucifix on the sanctuary wall right behind the altar. This crucifix is usually quite large and is well lit.

Being a Passionist, it is important to me that the symbol of our salvation and the love of God for us is displayed. For some time now, I have noticed one type of crucifix that I would like to comment on. It is the crucifix where the corpus is the body of the risen Christ. The cross is behind

Jesus and he is rising from it. This threw me at first. Why the resurrection and crucifixion together? Then I learned that theologically they are one event.

For example, when we celebrate the Triduum (Holy Thursday through Easter), although we are celebrating each day separately, they are one great mystery. Similarly, the death and resurrection of Jesus are one profound mysterious event. I like to say that resurrection life flows from the Passion. New life comes from the Cross of Jesus. The risen Jesus coming forth from the cross, although controversial to some, makes perfect sense to me. In the Cross of Jesus, resurrection life is available for the believer. It is not available only when we die! We can live the resurrected life now! I have a tape series available titled "Living the Resurrected Life." I love what Paul the Apostle wrote to his church at Philippi: "I want to know Jesus and the power that flows from his resurrection . . ." (Philippians 3:10) It is clear that powerful new life flows every day for the believer. It is this resurrected life flowing from the Passion that can help us live passionately.

WERE YOU THERE WHEN THEY . . . ?

I had the privilege of studying in the Holy Land during my theological studies in 1987. It was a three-month program that brought me to Greece, Turkey, Egypt, and Israel. What a thrill it was studying the Bible in the lands where it all took place! I will never forget the experience of God's grace during that study program. Since that time, I have had the opportunity to return to lead two pilgrimages. In 1995 I led 45 people to the Holy Land. More recently, in May of 1999, I led a pilgrimage with 33 others to Israel, Greece, and Rome. I love watching people experience the power of the land called "Holy".

I'd like to share something that happened to me during my study program in 1987. The Franciscans are guardians of many of the holy shrines in Israel. One of the most sacred churches is called the Church of the Holy Sepulcher in Jerusalem. This church is built over the place where scholars believe Jesus was crucified and raised. One day each week the church is locked shut for about three hours and closed to the public. Because I knew one of the Franciscans there, he allowed me to be in the church during that time of closure.

I was able to spend quiet time alone in prayer with my Bible on the hill called Golgotha or Calvary. It was a rock quarry at the time of Christ's death Today a pilgrim must ascend a number of stairs to get to the top of the large rock beneath the Church floor. At the top of the stairs, on the very site we believe Jesus was crucified, is an altar. Beneath this altar, there is an opening where pilgrims can reach in with their hand and actually touch the limestone rock beneath.

This site is normally packed with people going up and down the stairs and having their pictures taken. It can be noisy and very distracting. Absolutely no one else was present there for the hours I was there. I had it all to myself. I read the accounts of the crucifixion from the various Gospel writers, then prayed and tried to imagine the scene that occurred on that spot. I had a keen sense of the horror, pain, humiliation, desolation, and torture that occurred there.

Many books have been written trying to document what would happen during a crucifixion. I remember reading one such book in my theology training called *A Doctor at Calvary*. In this book, the author, a doctor, details what actually happened to the body during crucifixion. In horrifying detail, the author speaks of the pain, agony, and utter torture of crucifixion. Jesus would have hung there for three to six hours with nails through his wrists and feet piercing major nerves that would have caused intolerable pain. The pain was so intense and excruciating that those crucified would begin to blaspheme the onlookers as well as those who put them on the cross. All patience and character would be tested and tried beyond what could be endured. Every breath would be agony and effort. In the end, the legs of the victim would be broken so that he could not pull himself up to take another breath. The person crucified would die by asphyxiation. He would suffocate to death while every nerve in his body was screaming with unthinkable pain.

After I prayed and thought of these things, I went over to the place beneath the altar where the hole was. I was a seminarian at the time and as I knelt down, leaned over, and touched the rock beneath, I prayed, "Lord, I believe you are calling me to priesthood. I sense that you have called me. I believe one day I will be ordained and preach to many. Here I am, Lord. Send me. Anoint me with the words and the way to tell people what truly happened here. Grace me to proclaim the truth and the power of the sufferings of Jesus on our behalf. If I ever am to be ordained, gift me with the authority to preach Jesus and the meaning of this Cross for all . . ." It was a holy moment which I will never forget.

My life is dedicated to proclaiming the meaning of that event. I have vowed to do this. That is my mission in life. I embrace my call and try to live it passionately. I am utterly stupefied at what Jesus went through for us. Romans 5:8

proclaims the astounding fact that while we were *yet* sinners, Christ died for us. Someone gave me a card with a little metal cross attached that says, "While Christ was on the Cross, **you** were on his mind." Somehow, some way, in his divinity, Jesus thought of you while he was suffering.

The early Church made sense of the scandal of the Cross by proclaiming that through the event of a carpenter from Galilee being put to death by the Romans, sins are forgiven! How long it took them to come to this I do not know. I do know that I have found this to be absolutely true in my life. Isaiah the prophet spoke about this event hundreds of years before it ever took place.

> Surely he has borne our griefs and carried our sorrows; yet we esteemed him stricken, smitten by God, and afflicted. But he was wounded for *our transgressions*, he was bruised for *our iniquities*; upon him was the chastisement that made *us* whole, and with his stripes *we are healed*. We all like sheep have gone astray; we have turned every one to his own way; and the Lord has laid on him the iniquity *of us all*. (Isaiah 53:4-6)

As I minister across this land, I find people who are in need of all kinds of healing. There are many who are broken physically. Some have been scarred by the wounds of emotional abuse. Others are mentally ill. I believe the area where people most need a touch is in inner healing. Remember that Jesus was primarily a healer and the greatest healing event was the Cross. The word for salvation in Greek, *sozo*, also means healing. Many people need to be healed within, but each has to *want* to be healed.

Chapter 5

NORTH TO ALASKA!

I have many invitations to preach the Gospel in various churches around the United States. I was once invited to Pacific Palisades, California to share the Gospel with the people there. Pacific Palisades is just north of Los Angeles and has a fairly large and wealthy Catholic community. Because the community is large, I had a lot of Masses on the weekend and I was preaching at all of them.

I like to think that I preach enthusiastically and because of this, I get hungry often. Even when I eat a full meal right before an evening service, I will be hungry after the sermon. When people ask me how I stay so slim, I reply, "Preaching!" Because of this, in between two of the Masses on Sunday morning, I was in the kitchen looking for a cookie to tide me over for the next Mass. As I was searching, a man in his early seventies walked into the kitchen. It was the priest living in residence there whom I hadn't met yet.

"You must be Fr. Cedric," he said as he extended his hand to shake mine. "Yes I am," I replied. He introduced himself to me, then with a smile on his face said, "You're a young guy, people would love you . . . how'd you like to go on a cruise?" I thought he was just kidding. I said, "What do you mean?" He said, "I am the head chaplain for a number of cruise lines and priests from all over the world write to me asking me if they can be a chaplain on a cruise. I can send you anywhere in the world you want to go." Deep inside I'm thinking, "Wait a minute, I just came in here to get a cookie and he's offering me a cruise!" As I thought about it, I jokingly replied, "Well, I grew up in New England and have heard about the cruises to Alaska. That's where I'd like to go." Deep down, I thought to myself, "Nothing will ever happen."

DO YOU WANT TO BE HEALED?
(John 5:6)

Little did I know that one year later, I would be a chaplain on a five-star, top-of-the-line Crystal Cruise ship. (Before you go judging me, remember what Jesus taught . . . "Whoever leaves house or mother or father for my sake and for the Gospel will receive a hundredfold now in this time . . ." (Mark 10:29)) By the way, all expenses were paid! I had full guest status. I could dine with the passengers, dance, hot tub, swim, sauna, and go ashore when we docked. All I had to do was to preside at Eucharist once a day every morning.

One morning after I presided at Mass, I returned to my quarters and immediately heard a loud, quick knock at the door. As I opened the door, a man barged in and began pacing back and forth in my room. He never looked at me as he mumbled, "I know who you are. I've seen you with your priest collar on. I know you are the Catholic priest." "Sir," I said, "would you like to sit down?" "No," he said pacing. "I need to say something and this is not a confession. It is not a confession because quite frankly I am not able to change this situation that I am in. But I need to say this: I am in the midst of an adulterous relationship and it is tearing me up. I can't seem to do anything about it and it is so hard." Then he stopped pacing, looked at me for the first time and said, "You don't know how lucky you are!" I said, "Sir, please sit down for a few minutes and let's talk about it." "No!" he said as he began to head for the door, "I just needed to tell someone." Slam! The door shut behind him and I never saw him again.

That incident taught me a lot about sin. If ever a person should have had contentment and peace it would have been on that cruise to Alaska. There were bald eagles flying about. Whales spouted and danced by the ship. The glaciers and snow-capped mountains were out of a storybook. The food was heavenly and the entertainment was some of the best afloat. In the midst of this goodness, here was a man racked with torment, aflame with shame and guilt. He had no peace and was living a lie. "The wages of sin is death," the Bible teaches. You don't have to die physically to taste the death that the Bible talks about. Guilt is death. Shame is death. Separation from God is death.

If that man had sat down with me, I would have first talked about the awesome forgiveness of God. Since we were at sea, a perfect verse emphasizing that would have been Micah 7:19: "You will cast all our sins into the depths of the sea." Then I would have talked about the delivering power of God. God delivered the Hebrews through the sea. God can deliver us from anything we get ourselves into. I have learned that we may get ourselves into a bad situation that we can't get ourselves out of, *but God* can get us out of that situation. In fact, God will often teach us humility by allowing us to find out that we *can't* deliver ourselves from some things. Lessons like this teach us to lean on, rely on, and trust in God rather than other people or even ourselves.

If you are caught in a destructive relationship as you read this, I invite you right now to surrender yourself and the situation to God. Ask for deliverance and don't give up. It may look hopeless now, but in time, God will work it out for your good and will deliver you. If you are reading this and are considering adultery or even fantasizing about it, surrender yourself now. God will deliver you from a future of pain and shame. I wish I had the space to recount the stories I've heard of ruined lives and utter torment. Good people can allow themselves to be tempted, get trapped, and live in regret and misery.

I often pray for that man, because his mind was made up that things couldn't change in his life. My Bible says, "All things are possible for God!" (Mark 10:27) I've heard it said that there is a sign at Niagara Falls. It is about 100 yards from the edge of the falls where the millions upon millions of gallons of water come gushing over the cliff and crash down to the bottom below. On this sign are two words: "Beyond redemption." This man had the idea that somehow his case was "beyond redemption." No one is beyond redemption! No matter what situation you may be facing right now, whatever the sin, relationship, addiction, pattern, or brokenness you may be encountering, God is able to deliver you and redeem the situation! Trust God, believe him, surrender to him. God will act on your behalf!

CLEANSE ME FROM MY SIN
(Psalm 51:2)

Perhaps you are not dealing with anything as serious as adultery. I have discovered you don't have to be in serious sin to be pacing back and forth interiorly. This can happen in your own mind and heart with the little things of life. I call this the "Lexus Syndrome." The Lexus car manufacturers have an advertising slogan for their cars that they have used successfully for years. The slogan is: "The relentless pursuit of perfection."

We are not perfect. We all commit sins of gossip, lust, anger, pride, gluttony, sloth, and selfishness. Because we fail, we can spend hours, days, and even years beating ourselves up. Our conscience can be harsh and relentless toward us. We can pace back and forth in our own minds, distressed because we fall short. One of the most tragic truths I have encountered is that many people, even the best Christians, live in guilt and condemnation. They feel upset and distressed most of the time because they didn't behave perfectly. There is a "pall" hanging over them continuously.

When people live with guilt and condemnation, their relationship with the Lord suffers and this can color moods and attitudes toward themselves and others. The first thing that starts to go is a person's prayer life. I love what Hebrews 4:16 says about prayer: "Let us boldly and confidently draw near to the throne of grace that we may receive mercy and find grace to help in time of need." It's hard to pray, let alone come boldly before God, when we are feeling imperfect and condemning ourselves.

The writer of Hebrews was talking about this very situation in Hebrews 4:14-16. The author was saying that Jesus is our great high priest, one who can sympathize with our weaknesses. Jesus was tempted. He knows how we feel. It is *through him, with him* and *in him* that we can come before the throne of grace (undeserved favor) for mercy (forgiveness and healing). Notice we come not in our own good or bad behavior, not in our own righteousness, but in Christ. The writer of Hebrews is *encouraging* us, no matter how we feel about ourselves, to come to Christ in prayer and we will be helped.

THE PRECIOUS BLOOD

A little later on in Hebrews 9:14 we read, "How much more shall the blood of Christ, who through the eternal Spirit offered himself without blemish to God, purify your conscience from dead works to serve the living God." It is the blood of Jesus that cleanses! There is a whole religious community in the Catholic Church whom God raised up called the Precious Blood. The blood of Jesus is *precious* and *powerful*! You must know that the purpose of the blood is to cleanse our consciences and hearts from feeling guilty and condemning ourselves. If evil tries to remind you of your unworthiness and make you feel guilty because of your transgressions, claim the blood. Go to a crucifix, touch it and say, "Jesus, I know you died for me. Cleanse me of guilt and condemnation by your precious blood." Lay your burdens down! When talking about the accusing power of Satan, the Bible says in Revelation 12:11, "They conquered him by the blood of the lamb."

Always remember that Satan is the "accuser of men and women." Satan is a liar and he will constantly accuse you. The same devil who tempts you to sin then heaps guilt and condemnation on you for the sin you fell into! He'll tell you you're not good enough. He'll try to make you give up. Victorious living comes through the blood of the lamb.

When I lived in Missouri years ago, I was involved in youth ministry. Once I heard about a blood drive they were having at our parish and went to donate. As I was sitting there the nurse put the needle into my arm and told me to squeeze the piece of wood that she put in my hand. As I was squeezing, I watched the blood flow out of my arm into the sack beneath. All of a sudden, I didn't feel very good. I began to feel faint and started getting woozy. The nurse became aware of it and laid me down and later gave me some juice and a cookie to help me regain strength. It was as if when my blood flowed out of me, my strength and life left, too.

The biblical ancients thought that the soul and life of a person resided in the blood. (Leviticus 17:11) Blood was and is valuable and precious. When we talk about the blood of Jesus, we are talking about his very life poured out for us. It was for a reason–so we could be cleansed! No wonder we are given the opportunity to come into communion with the blood every day if we want to. We need constant cleansing from feelings of guilt and condemnation. The "dead works" in Hebrews 9:14 are attempts to make up for our guilt by our own deeds or efforts.

I have found that many people beat themselves up to try to make up for their sins. If I beat myself up for whatever length of time, some people reason, then God will accept me. That is not how it works. You can never "make up" for any wrong you have done in your life. Isaiah makes the bold statement that "all our righteous deeds are like a polluted garment." (Isaiah 64:6) You are right with God only ***"in Christ."*** The phrase "in Christ" is found in many places in the New Testament. It is how God sees us, through our baptism into Christ and our faith in him.

The idea of a penance given in reconciliation, for example, is not to punish you so you can somehow "make up" for what you did wrong. Rather a penance given you by the priest is an action to *bring you to Jesus*. The priest is trying to help you realize your position in Christ. You are forgiven. You are favored. You are right with God in Christ. It does no good to remain guilty and full of self-condemnation. You must learn to be gentle with yourself. You must accept yourself as you are. I like to say, "I'm OK and I'm on my way!" I saw a bumper sticker that read, "Christians aren't perfect, just forgiven."

Please don't get me wrong. I am in no way saying not to strive for perfection. However, realistically, there are going to be some times that we fall and fail. You must accept yourself as you are and be good and kind to yourself as you struggle in the spiritual life. God is doing a great work in you. God will help you. You must help yourself, too.

Also, you must understand that guilt can be good. It is a natural response that God puts in us (and that we learn) to help us be aware of wrongdoing. Guilt certainly can be a great motivator! But know that people can also "harden their hearts" by denying the guilt they feel. If this happens over and over, a person becomes insensitive to the convicting grace of the Holy Spirit and can spiral downwards spiritually. The famous verse in the Bible illustrating this is: "If today you hear the voice of the Lord, harden not your hearts." (Hebrews 3:7,13) While there are many who have become deaf to the Spirit's prompting in this area, many others are feeling guilty without needing to.

TO ALL WHO RECEIVED HIM . . .
(John 1:12)

You must understand this. We are saved and cleansed by the blood of Jesus. If you are constantly feeling guilty and beating yourself up all the time, you are not trusting in the blood. If you are trying to make up for your sins, you are not relying on the blood. If you believe that you are forgiven, but deep down haven't forgiven yourself, you don't understand the blood. If there is some confessed, deep, dark secret from your past that haunts you in the back of your mind, you aren't trusting in the blood. Of course when I talk about the blood, I mean the blood sacrifice of Jesus. What I am saying here can be liberating and life-changing for you. You can and must accept his pardon in your life.

In 1829, a man named George Wilson robbed the U.S. mail and committed a murder in the act. He was later arrested, tried, convicted, and sentenced to be hanged. Some of his friends petitioned President Andrew Jackson for a pardon. Though that pardon was granted, Wilson refused to accept it! This was a strange situation. Eventually, the matter came before the U.S. Supreme Court. In their decision, Justice Marshall explained that in order to be valid, a pardon must be accepted by the condemned person. While it is virtually inconceivable that a person sentenced to death would refuse a pardon, that person had the right to do so. George Wilson was executed while his written pardon lay on the sheriff's desk.

I have found that as I trust in his pardon and forgiveness for me, God actually heals the guilt. Whenever I pray the Stations of the Cross, I am always struck by the first station. Jesus is condemned. Once, Jesus stood before a Roman procurator and was condemned unjustly. I believe that he stood there for me. Now I trust in the liberating words of Romans 8:1: "There is therefore now *no condemnation* for those who are in Christ Jesus." I have heard that verse set to song and it is music to my ears! You might even want to say those words out loud over and over. Because of his pardon, I am able to forgive myself. I find that I can pray with boldness. I don't beat myself up because I'm not perfect. I forget what lies behind and press on to what lies ahead. You can too. Jesus was condemned for you. Accept the pardon!

Many people have trouble forgiving themselves. I have discovered that there is no substitute for searching the Word of God yourself. You can have a priest tell you to forgive yourself and you don't. However, when you search on your own and read the Scriptures yourself, something powerful happens. The Word with "inbuilt" power starts to work in you. Recently, I went to confession and then read Psalm 85. As I read about God forgiving the sin of his people and restoring peace to his people, I received peace and restoration. I forgave myself and moved on. Faith comes by hearing and, in this case, hearing comes by simply reading the Word. Do you know what the Bible says about forgiveness or do you just rely on your own thoughts?

WHO HAS BELIEVED WHAT WE HAVE HEARD? (Isaiah 53:1)

As I said before, I am a Passionist priest and religious. Along with ministering and serving, my primary call is reflection on God and growing in Christ. Our first vow is to meditate on the Passion of Christ and to proclaim its meaning to all. I am dedicated to this vow which I professed publicly in 1985. I have spent many hours in prayer reflecting and meditating on the sufferings and death of Jesus. Our founder, St. Paul of the Cross, stated that meditating on the cross is the greatest way to holiness and mystical union with God. His missionaries were to teach the people how to meditate on the cross. This was so important, that each mission would have time set apart for such instruction.

Many of you are Passionists without even knowing it! I believe our charism (gift) to the Church is the central gift of the Church. If you ever pray the sorrowful mysteries of the rosary, you are delving into the Passionist charism. Meditating on the Stations of the Cross is concentrating on Jesus' sufferings. Reading a book about Jesus' Passion, gazing at a crucifix, watching a movie about Christ are all ways to reflect on the pains Jesus endured.

I must admit that many times I get distracted when I reflect on the sufferings of Jesus and meditate on the Passion. But there are times when I see Jesus hanging there, writhing in pain, panting, and suffering in silent torture. It is absolutely clear to me that he was offering himself to God on our behalf. Jesus was pouring out his love for us.

Paul the apostle makes a radical statement in Galatians 2:21: "I do not nullify the grace of God; for if justification (being made right with God) were through the law (our own efforts and works), then Christ died to no purpose." Wow! He is saying that if you try to justify yourself by your own efforts, you are actually going against God's plan of the Cross! If we take this thought a bit further, I'd like to say, don't negate the value and worth of Christ's sacrifice for you by trying to make up for your own sins or to win God's pardon by feeling guilty. Only Jesus can save you and cleanse you.

Romans 3:25 makes it clear that God put Jesus forward as an expiation by his blood, to be *received by faith*. That is the key. You must release your faith in the blood of Jesus and its cleansing power. It is interesting that in the book of Exodus the Israelites were told to *apply the blood* on the doorpost so the destroyer would "pass over" them. (Exodus 12:22,23) In the same way we must apply the blood of Jesus on the doorpost of our hearts and consciences, as it were, to experience the cleansing that his blood brings. You do this by faith. Trust that the valuable, precious blood of the spotless lamb of God can cleanse you of all guilt and deliver you from sin. You will be purified from "dead works" to serve the living God!

I love to preside at the Eucharist. I remember when I studied the development of Eucharist and its history in the seminary. Each part of the Mass can be broken down and has meaning in and of itself. Much of it is symbolic. One of my favorite parts of the Mass is what is called the "Doxology." This is when the priest elevates the host and cup and says or sings, "Through him, with him and in him, in the unity of the Holy Spirit, all glory and honor are yours almighty Father forever and ever." Then comes the great Amen.

What is the priest doing at that moment? Proclaiming in words or song how the Christian life is to be lived. Not through ourselves, with us, or in self, but rather, through, with, and in **Christ**. It is "in Christ" that we must live and give glory to God. Notice also that the priest holds up the blood. This is very symbolic. It is through the blood that we are forgiven. It is with the blood that we are cleansed. It is in the blood that we are purified. Confession is one of the ways we can increase our faith in the saving blood of Jesus, and Eucharist is another. Paying close attention to sacred moments such as these can grace and help you.

There is a story in Mark's Gospel that demonstrates for me what a sacrament can be. It is the story of the woman who had a flow of blood for twelve years. (Mark 5:25-34) She was bleeding inside. We don't know the cause of her pain, but we know her cure: Jesus. When she *touched* Jesus, she experienced healing. Power and virtue flowed from Jesus because of her faith. Many people were touching Jesus at that moment, but she received because she came in faith. Jesus applauded her faith as he told her in verse 34, "Daughter, your faith has made you well; go in peace and be healed."

When you come to communion, come to receive all that Jesus died to give you. You have already prayed in faith, "Lord, I am not worthy to receive you, but only say the word and I shall be **healed**." As you come to drink the blood of Jesus from the cup, touch Jesus by thinking, "Cleanse me Lord, heal me, only say the word, I trust in your blood!" That's releasing your faith! That's receiving! The woman healed of the issue of blood *said to herself*, "If I only touch his garment I shall be made well."(Matthew 9:21) This is the way to receive a sacrament–*actively.* Remember, a sacrament is an encounter with the risen Jesus and a touch of grace. We touch him and he touches us! If you want to live passionately, you must experience cleansing from guilt and condemnation. Otherwise, you will be living in harassing torment.

BY HIS STRIPES WE ARE HEALED
(Isaiah 53:5)

As I write this book, I am stationed at Christ the King Passionist Retreat Center in Sacramento. Sacramento is not the largest city in California. Los Angeles and San Francisco are certainly bigger. But Sacramento (named after the Blessed Sacrament) is the capital city. There is a large capitol building downtown and many legislators work there each day.

One day in January 1993 I read something in the newspaper. It was the 20th anniversary of the Roe v. Wade decision which legalized abortion in the United

States. There was a pro-life rally planned for the steps of the capitol building that day. I had never been to such a rally and since I had some time thought I would go. I dressed in my blue jeans and golf shirt so no one would know that I was a priest.

When I got there, I saw about 1,000 people on one side of the building. They looked very peaceable. Many were holding roses, some had babies at their breast and they seemed very quiet and orderly. These were the pro-life people. On the other side of the building I saw about 75 people. Some were holding coat hangers and beating drums and making a lot of noise. These were the pro-choice people. I thought to myself, "I'm going back over to the pro-life people, they are full of peace."

I noticed that there was a platform set up on the upper stairs with a microphone. I figured the organizers of the event were going to speak and cheerlead the cause. About four women proceeded to the platform and began speaking, one at a time. What I heard next was shocking. They were all women who had had abortions. They were sharing their stories in front of all those people.

Each one talked about the tragedy and trials of having an abortion. They spoke of the selfishness involved and how they acted out of convenience. One at a time, they spoke about the shame, guilt, and inner hate that occurred after the procedure. They felt like monsters and believed they had committed the "unpardonable" sin. Each one of them had trouble living with herself and forgiving herself.

Then something happened that touched me deeply. I've been to a lot of religious services all around this country. Some have been in Protestant churches, others in charismatic circles, and I've conducted many of them myself. This gathering suddenly became very religious. What I heard next made me weep. Each one of the women talked about how in her desperation and pain, she came to Jesus. They each asked for forgiveness. Each one received a healing touch from Christ. They spoke of how Jesus took away the awful guilt, shame and pain of their deeds and set them free to forgive themselves for what they did. One of them jumped up and down in her witness and shouted, "Jesus set me free!"

I don't know if they were Catholic or not, but I do know they were saved. They were walking miracles and a testimony to what God can do in a person's life. What am I saying here? NO MATTER the sin–abortion, adultery, lying, cheating, stealing, killing, anger, gossip, lust, laziness, or whatever else you may be involved in–it is forgiven at the cross!

FATHER, FORGIVE ME FOR I HAVE SINNED . . .

Many times a woman (or man) who has heard me preach about this will come into the confessional and for the first time confess that she had had an abortion or she (he) helped someone get an abortion. The guilt feelings are intense. Many out there are afraid to come to confession fearing what the priest might say. Others are beating themselves up constantly and living with inner torment. That is just what the evil one wants for you: guilt and torment. One of the most inspiring verses in the whole of the Bible is this one: "Come to me all you who labor and are heavy laden, and I will give you rest." (Matthew 11:28) Jesus will never turn you away. Come just as you are. That is the only way you *can* come. It is my hope that those of you out there who have had serious unconfessed sin in your life will seek out reconciliation. The time is NOW! You've been hurting too long. Jesus wants to give you rest. You long for this. Receive it!

The power of the sacrament of reconciliation has been one of the greatest surprises of my ministry. I continue to marvel at the vulnerability of the people when they come to me. Burdens are laid down. People are set free. Christ touches his people and brings blessing. The emphasis in this sacrament now is on healing. Simply come in faith, and the Master will touch you and heal you within. St. Paul of the Cross, the founder of the Passionists and a great preacher, stated that the object of his preaching was to move people to come to confession!

I have heard the stories of thousands of people. Sometimes I hear things that are shameful and distressing for people to tell. I marvel at how with the words "I absolve you from your sins" and with the sign of the cross, even the worst sins are forgiven and wiped clean. Sometimes I think, "Wow, it seems like after all that person did, something more should happen to make them be forgiven." But I know the *gold* behind the sign of the cross and the words of absolution. That gold is the suffering, shed blood and death of Jesus on the Cross. No other price needs to be paid. Nothing else is good enough. Beating yourself up for the rest of your life isn't going to do it. Jesus simply wants you to come in faith and accept and receive his sacrifice for you personally.

It is important to understand that the *priest* does not forgive your sins. What we do is celebrate with you the forgiveness that was *already won* for you at Calvary. We "minister" this forgiveness to you. The celebration of the sacrament helps you to "receive" and accept a healing touch from Christ. This touch can give you the grace to forgive yourself, help you to lay down the guilt and shame, then go forward with your life. The grace that Jesus offers can actually set you free to overcome any particular habitual sin with which you struggle. One of the benefits of confession is to empower you to live in freedom.

I heard a story about a mother who was trying to get her eight-year-old daughter to go to confession. No matter what she tried to say, the little girl was determined not to go. "C'mon honey; Father is nice; go to confession," the mother cajoled. "Nope, I'm not going to confession," said the girl. "Why? Father will help you so don't be afraid. It will be OK." "Nope," said the little girl. "C'mon, go!" said the mother. "NO!" came the reply. "Why not?" asked the mother. Then the little girl replied, "Because the last time I went to confession, Father told me to pray three Hail Mary's . . . and I only know one!"

A hallmark of the New Covenant is this stunning statement: "I will remember your sins no more." (Hebrews 8:12) I have a boom box with a cassette player. When I put a cassette in, I can record favorite songs from the radio. Later, if I want to record another song over the previously recorded song, I back the tape up and press play/record and suddenly the new song is recorded over the old one. Or, if I want a blank tape again, I back the tape up and simply press play/record with no radio on. Immediately a blank tape appears. God can erase the tape! Somehow, someway, God has the ability to forget the wrong we have done. God is very old and has "senior moments" in regard to our wrongdoing. I call it "sin Alzheimers."

It's like the story of an elderly couple who were sitting on the couch watching TV. Suddenly the husband got a hankering for a ham and cheese sandwich. "I'm going to the kitchen for a ham and cheese sandwich," he said to his wife. "Great," she replied, "make me one too, and put mayonnaise on it." "I will," he said. "Better write it down," his wife said. "I won't forget," he said as he entered the kitchen.

About ten minutes later the man came into the living room with a banana split for his wife. "Here you go honey," he said. Viewing the recently made banana split the wife said, "I told you to write it down, you forgot the whipped cream!"

We may remember what we have done wrong, but God forgets. "As far as east is from west, so far has God put our transgressions from us." (Psalm 103:12) God is amazingly generous in forgiveness and as we trust in the Cross, we will be cleansed and purified from guilt also. We may remember what we have done wrong, but there will be no punch of guilt or sting of condemnation. When you're absolved, it dissolves.

There are many reasons why people don't come to reconciliation. Some are afraid, others don't know how to do it, still others fear that the priest might say something because they haven't been in a long time! My personal record is someone who hadn't been to reconciliation in over 60 years. Let me tell you a secret–priests love to hear confessions like that! We're not going to yell at you. We are in the business of conversion. Jesus called us fishers of men and women. We call people like that "big fish." No matter how long it has been or what you've done, don't let fear keep you away. You will be so glad once you come! Lay your burdens down. Don't let Satan tempt you into staying away. Let the Lord heal you. God is compassionate and God's mercy is new every day. (Lamentations 3:22-23)

6
UNION WITH GOD
"The Passion still remains the door through which the soul enters into union with God."
(St. Paul of the Cross)

THIS IS ETERNAL LIFE . . .
(John 17:3)

If you want to live passionately, you must **know** God. This is a reality that absolutely turned my life upside down and inside out and changed me as a Catholic Christian. I grew up knowing *about* God but never really having an active, vital, living relationship with God in Jesus Christ. I wasn't even sure that this was possible. Yet, along with forgiveness, this is another of the hallmarks of the New Covenant, "And they shall not teach every one his fellow or every one her sister, saying, 'Know the Lord,' for **all shall know me** from the least of them to the greatest." (Hebrews 8:11) This is God's great desire for his people: that we know him in a personal way. What a thrilling reality it is to live each day in intimacy with the living God.

The Hebrew word for knowing, *yadah*, means more than knowing about some type of object. Rather, it means to enter into a personal, intimate relationship with someone. In the Old Testament, we read that so and so "knew" his wife and they had a child. That implies oneness and intimacy. The prophet Hosea said that his people suffer from a lack of knowledge of God. (Hosea 4:6) This meant if you are not intimate with God, your life will be poverty stricken and you will suffer separation from God.

Similarly in the New Testament, the Gospel writer John used the Greek word, *gnoskein*, for knowing. When he used that word, he was talking about involvement between two subjects. To know someone means to encounter them and to entrust yourself to that person with your mind, will and emotions. It is a personal relationship. A little known verse that is one of my favorites is John 17:3. "This is eternal life, that they **know** you the only true God and Jesus Christ whom you have sent." In other words, eternal life has a "nowness" to it. It is a new quality of life. It is the richness of having a relationship with God. This is one of the deepest senses of what it means to live passionately.

It is absolutely crucial for you to understand you can experience God every day. Certainly you understand that you can encounter God through a sunrise and a sunset, at the shores of the ocean or the foothills of the snow-capped mountains. God can be seen in a rose or baby's face. God also comes to us through people, sacraments, art work, music and the Bible. This is God's *mediated* presence coming though creation.

In addition, there is God's *unmediated* presence alive in your heart. This is the presence of the Holy Spirit living in you. You can know and have fellowship with God every day in an unmediated way through awareness and prayer. It is important for you to know that **you** can know God and develop intimacy with God in your life!

THE LORD IS MY SHEPHERD
(Psalm 23)

I once heard a story about a young man who was studying in the seminary to be a minister. He was renowned for his ability to memorize scriptures and proclaim them without notes. One day, he came home on spring break and was present for the Sunday service. When the pastor saw that he was in the congregation, he called him forward and said, "Young man, these folks are in need of some inspiration. Would you please proclaim Psalm 23 to them?"

Up stepped this 22-year-old young man. He stood in front of the congregation and a hush came over the community. He began loudly, "The Lord is my Shepherd. I shall not want. He makes me lie down in green pastures. He leads me beside still waters. He refreshes my soul. Even though I walk through the valley of the shadow of death, I fear no evil, for you are with me; with your rod and your staff that give me comfort!" Everyone looked at this young whippersnapper with admiration and thought, "What is he going to be? He'll be an amazing preacher!"

Just then a man in the second pew raised his hand and the pastor called on him. "Pastor," he said, "Can we hear her do it?" as he pointed to the woman seated next to him. The woman next to him was a blind 86-year-old woman. "Sure" said the pastor, "Come on up!" and the woman hobbled forward.

It took her some time to get to the sanctuary, but finally she stood there with her cane, barely looked up and began in a soft, shaky, confident voice: "The Lord is my shepherd. I shall not want. He makes me lie down in green pastures. He leads me beside still waters. He refreshes my soul." Then with tears in her eyes, she began to look up. "Even though I walk through the valley of darkness I fear no evil, for you are with me; with your rod and staff that gives me comfort." You could have heard a pin drop in that church when the woman finished.

The young seminarian suddenly got up and went over to the pastor. "God just spoke to me," he said. "You see, I know the Psalm, but she *knows the shepherd*!"

The good news is that we are not alone! Always remember you are never alone. No matter what you are going through, God is there for you. Whatever darkness or valley of death you are experiencing in your life, you have a shepherd who is with you and wants to comfort you. Perhaps you lost a loved one to death and are feeling lonely. It could be that you are stressed and worried about the future. Perhaps you are in despair and depressed about your life. Maybe you are dealing with a health problem. The glorious truth is that Jesus is there to walk you through it and to help you. He is the Good Shepherd who will never leave his sheep. One of the purposes of trials and tribulations is to help us to learn to trust and lean on Jesus.Storms can actually bring us to deeper faith if we will let them.

I AM THE DOOR
(John 10:9)

Something very curious happened at the moment of Jesus' death. It is recorded in Mark 15:38, "And behold, the curtain of the temple was torn in two, from top to bottom." Why would Mark record such an event? What is the significance of this "curtain"? (Matthew and Luke record this event also, with varying significance depending on their particular purpose.)

In order to understand, we need to take a quick look at the Temple itself. The temple in Jerusalem at the time of Jesus was rebuilt by King Herod the Great. First built by King Solomon, then rebuilt at the time of the return of the exiles from Babylon, the Herodian temple at the time of Jesus would have been larger than the original temple.

Surrounding the temple proper was a large area called the Court of the Gentiles (non-Jews). Anyone could enter this area. Then, as you entered the temple itself you first stepped into the Court of the Women. As you went further on you entered the Court of Israel. Deeper still was the Court of the Priests. Then you came upon the Holy Place and finally, separated by a curtain, was the Holy of Holies. Originally the Holy of Holies contained the Ark of the Covenant, a 4 ft. by 2.5 ft. by 4 ft. box carried on two poles. Inside were the two tablets of the law from Mt. Sinai. Above the ark was the gold "mercy seat." It was thought that the *shekinah* (Glory of God in cloud form) dwelt above the mercy seat. On either side of the ark was a cherubim angel. By the time of Jesus, the Holy of Holies was an empty room, but it was believed that the *shekinah* presence of God still dwelt there.

An interesting point to note is that Gentiles were not permitted beyond the Court of the Gentiles. In fact, archeologists have found a stone marker inscribed in Latin and Greek warning foreigners of the death penalty for trespassing. They were not even allowed to enter into the outermost Court of the Women lest they defile the temple.

Once a year on the Day of Atonement, one person, the High Priest, would go beyond the curtain and enter the Holy of Holies with incense and the blood of a bull and goat, and he would apply the blood to the mercy seat. This ritualistic action was to "atone" for his sins as well as the sins of the people.

At the moment Jesus died, there was a cosmic rip. The temple curtain was torn from top to bottom.

I fly a lot on airplanes. When I am able, I like to get the seat right behind first class. This bulkhead seat offers more leg room than most seats, especially when you sit on the aisle. One thing you can't miss is that right after takeoff the flight attendant comes to unfasten the curtain and she pulls it closed so that at times it hits my leg. The purpose of this curtain? It *separates* first class from coach!

When Jesus died the curtain was torn. Scholars interpret this in a number of ways, but the most meaningful for me is that now there is no separation between us and God! No longer do we need a high priest to go into the inner sanctuary once a year on our behalf. Once and for all Jesus, our great High Priest, has entered into Heaven itself with his own blood so that we can be cleansed and have access to God. (Hebrews 10:19-22) Please understand: because of the sacrificial death of Jesus, a new age of grace has dawned and *anyone and everyone has access to God*! There is no longer any separation.

When I grew up, I attended a large, anonymous Catholic church in Springfield, Massachusetts. We hardly knew anyone and it seemed like everything was done "through the priest." There was an altar rail that seemed to separate people from the sanctuary and I understood that I could only come to God through the priest. Now, while it is true that you can only celebrate most sacraments if a priest is present, you do not need a priest in order to come to God. You can have access on your own. **You** have access to God every bit as much as any priest or the Pope himself for that matter. God is an "equal opportunity employer," as it were. He shows no partiality and is just toward everyone.

Sometimes people will tell me that I have a special "hotline" to God because I am a priest. I tell them that they have the same access that I do. The truth about calling God is that his line is never busy, God never puts you on hold and you never get an answering machine. It is not a long-distance call and it is always toll free. In fact, God has call-waiting. He is always waiting for your call!

At one time the Gentiles couldn't even come into the Court of the Israelite women under penalty of death! The stone sign said "No trespassing!" Now, in Christ, the sign in front of the Holy of Holies says, *"All are welcome!"*

Make no mistake about this. You are no longer separated from God. You have access! The whole feast of Epiphany which we celebrate during the Christmas season shouts this reality. God's secret plan was for the Gentiles and Jews to be co-heirs of God. Come boldly before the throne in Christ. There is no longer any class distinction. The curtain has been torn. I love Galatians 3:28. "There is neither Jew nor Greek, there is neither slave nor free, there is neither male nor female; for you are all one in Christ Jesus."

In 70 A.D. the Jewish Temple was finally destroyed by the Romans. The center of Jewish religion and the place of pilgrimage was leveled. No longer was there an earthly Holy of Holies. Paul questioned his Corinthian community and us when he asked, "Do you not know that **you** are God's temple and that God's Spirit dwells in you?" (1 Corinthians 3:16) We are the new temple. No mere building alone can contain God. God's shekinah glory dwells in us. Our heart has become the Holy of Holies on earth. Reverence God in your heart. Respect your body. You can be as close to God as you want to be. I saw a sign in a pastor's office in Jacksonville, Florida: "If you feel distant from God, who made the first move away?"

† Part II †

The Transforming Power of the Cross

7
CRUCIFIED WITH JESUS
"I desire to know nothing else nor to taste any consolation; my sole desire is to be crucified with Jesus." (St. Paul of the Cross)

I HAVE BEEN CRUCIFIED WITH CHRIST
(Galatians 2:20)

We Passionists begin our morning prayer everyday of our lives with these words: "At the name of Jesus, every knee must bend, in the heavens, on earth, and under the earth, and every tongue confess that Jesus Christ is Lord." (Philippians 2:10-11) This phrase comes from an ancient liturgical hymn well known to many today. What precedes it is what I want to focus on: "Have this mind among yourselves, which is yours in Christ Jesus, who, though he was in the form of God, did not count equality with God a thing to be grasped, but emptied himself, taking the form of a servant, being born in the likeness of people. And being found in human form he humbled himself and became obedient unto death, even death on a cross." (Philippians 2:5-8)

We have a very beautiful chapel at Christ the King retreat center in Sacramento. Groups come from all over seeking a deeper walk with Christ. Once we sponsored an R.C.I.A. (Rite of Christian Initiation of Adults) workshop. They put a large cross right in the middle of the chapel floor. It was about 10 feet high and had no corpus on it.

One evening when the chapel was empty, I went and saw the cross standing there. I approached it and looked at the front of it. Because it was in the center of the floor,

I was able to walk around it. I noticed something: the cross has two sides. Usually it is on a wall or hung somewhere and its other side is hard to notice. As I looked at the back side of the cross, I heard a tiny whisper in me. I believe it was the still small voice of the Holy Spirit. "The front side of the cross was for Jesus, the back side of the cross is for you." I am still learning what that means . . .

CONFRONT THE CROSS

If you want to live passionately, you must embrace the cross. Jesus was extremely obedient. He humbled himself. He emptied himself. Because of this, God highly exalted him. Jesus made these same radical demands on his followers. This teaching wasn't to make our lives difficult, but rather, so that we would discover new life. "If anyone would come after me, let him deny himself and take up his cross and follow me. For whoever would save his life will lose it; and whoever loses his life for my sake and the gospel's will save it. For what does it profit a person, to gain the whole world and forfeit his life?" (Mark 8:34-36)

I have come to realize a stunning truth about my life. My whole life is a process of being crucified with Christ. "I have been crucified with Christ; it is no longer I who live but Christ who lives in me." (Galatians 2:20) When we were baptized and came to trust Christ as Lord, something very mystical happened. We were crucified on the cross with him. We were united with him in his death. "Do you not realize," Paul asks, "that all of us who have been baptized into Christ Jesus were baptized into his death?" (Romans 6:2) This is how God sees us, one with Christ in his death. We are crucified with Christ. This is ours *legally*.

However, *experientially*, I am *being* crucified. The "I" that I am talking about here is the sinful, wayward, prideful self. No matter how good I think I am, there is a part of me that is rebellious and controlling. The middle letter in the word sin and pride is: "I". This is the self we must "deny." We must "empty" ourselves of our self. To take up our cross means radical obedience to God. It means dying to my wants and living for others. It means putting God and God's ways first. The sinful self (what the Bible calls the flesh) must be crucified. Realities such as moodiness, harshness, cynicism, being judgmental, wayward thoughts and imaginings, an unbridled tongue, independence from God, and bad attitudes must die. This "dying" is the process of sanctification. We must die to live!

"I die every day," Paul said in 1 Corinthians 15:31. He was talking about his sufferings in obedience to Christ. In order for us to follow Christ the way he demands, our selfish attitudes must die. We must learn to choose correctly and not be dominated by the way we feel. Are you moody and harsh toward others? Are you optimistic and positive? Are you quick to forgive? Do you try to control people? Are you moldable and pliable in God's hands? Do you reach out and serve others? God is looking for people who are extremely obedient.

Obedience includes keeping the commandments, but is so much more. It is a life-style of saying "Yes" to God, over and over again. It is "taking up" the cross daily and living with the charism of the Passion at the center of your being. The Cross becomes internalized. You become motivated by giving and selflessness rather than selfishness. Your attitudes toward people and life change. You trust God and depend on him rather than on yourself. You become transformed. John the Baptist said it best, "Jesus must increase and I must decrease." (John 3:30) That is a prime principle for passionate living!

8
HUMILITY LEADS TO GLORY
"When will we be so humble that we will consider it our glory to be the outcast of the people?"
(St. Paul of the Cross)

COUNT IT ALL JOY
(James 1:2)

I was ordained a priest on June 29, 1991. The Gospel proclaimed at my ordination was Luke 4:16-21. It had to do with the "Spirit of the Lord" anointing Jesus to preach, release, heal, and liberate people. When Jesus quoted these verses from Isaiah 61 at his hometown in Nazareth, something went drastically wrong. For a while they listened with admiration. But Jesus had a vision for breaking boundaries and reaching out to the entire world. The citizens of this small Galilean village couldn't handle this broad vision and rose up against Jesus with wrath. Luke 4:29-30 reads, "And they rose up and put him out of the city, and led him to the brow of the hill on which their city was built, that they might throw him down headlong. But passing through the midst of them he went away."

Notice that Jesus was almost put to death right away. They wanted to throw him over the cliff and kill him! These were his own townspeople! This scene at the beginning of the public ministry in Luke is a foreshadowing of what was to come for Jesus. Jesus would endure misunderstanding, envy, anger, hatred, and would eventually suffer death at the hands of unjust people.

What blesses me is the next verse. If you don't read between the lines, you might miss it. "And he went down to Capernaum, a city of Galilee. And he was teaching them on the Sabbath . . ." (Luke 4:31) *Immediately after* they tried to kill him, Jesus was at it again. The whole thing could have ended right there. Jesus could have said, "This is too much for me, I'm giving up." But Jesus kept pressing on, no matter what. What resilience! What an attitude of determination! Jesus was not the type to give up.

If you want to live passionately, you must have the ability to "bounce back" quickly from trials and adversity. We all have people, situations and events that come against us. This is common to everybody. It is a person's ability to handle these situations well that determines how far that person will go in life. Are you giving up or going up? It all depends on your attitude.

Early in my career, before I met the Passionists, I was a youth minister in a small town in Northern Missouri. The town of Marceline is a town of about 3,000 people. I spent one year there (1981) teaching young people in the school, visiting elderly, publishing a newsletter and helping liturgically. One aspect of my ministry that excited me was door to door evangelization. I had been given a list of names of people who, for whatever reason, had fallen away from the Church and were no longer attending Sunday Mass. I had the ministry of visiting these people with the intent of inviting them back.

This was a very hard ministry. I was knocking on their doors, asking to be invited in to their space and talking about religion. Primarily I was not there to argue or to discuss. Rather, as an ambassador of Jesus and of our local church, I was there to invite them back. I was met with interesting responses.

I'll never forget the time I knocked on the door of one house and after identifying myself as the youth minister at the Church, I was allowed to enter. The people there were a man and his wife in their fifties. They seemed nice enough and I basically talked to them, told them where I was from and tried to engage them in small talk. Then, I told them why I was there. I invited them to attend Mass on Sunday. When I said this, the man changed his facial appearance and said to me, "I'm not going to be going back to Church on Sunday and if I ever do, you wouldn't be the type of guy that would attract me back." That hurt. I gingerly made some more small talk and then made my way to the door. I couldn't help but feel tears well up in my eyes after that visit. I felt rejected and discounted as a person. I was only trying to help and be a blessing in their life and they wanted nothing of it.

SHAKE IT OFF!

That was one of my first rejections as a minister. I didn't give up. I continued to visit other homes and to serve as a youth minister. Jesus told his missionaries, "If they do not receive you, say, 'even the dust that clings to our feet we wipe off against you.'" (Luke 10:10-11) In other words, shake it off! Don't take it personally. When they rejected me, they were actually rejecting Jesus. The temptation is to step into the swirl of self-pity and self-doubt and stay there awhile. I have found that I can be resilient in Christ.

The times that I am not on the road preaching I am home living community life. I live in a small community of about eight or nine men in Sacramento. Every once in a while we have community meetings. I have found that I do not always see eye to eye with the men I live with. When we are talking about an issue, often I will seem to be in the minority. At times I will sense antagonism and resistance toward my views. Often I don't get what I want. When that happens I used to spend a long time in self doubt and self pity. Now, I have learned to shake it off and go on. It is not life and death. We can't always get what we want. That is part of the sanctification process of community life, and marriage for that matter. We cannot control life and have all people and things exactly the way we want them!

The ministry God has called me to is a rewarding ministry. I have the privilege of ministering to tens of thousands of people each year. I travel the country and meet lots of saints throughout this land; however, ministry has its difficulties.

Every weekend that I am on the road, I must get up before a new congregation with a new message and "call" them to the mission. The goal of the weekend homily is to get people to come to the rest of the mission (Monday through Wednesday). I know what the percentages are before I even get up there. I am aware from past experience that even the best missionaries, no matter how good they are, will only get about one third of the people to come. Most of the percentages are less. In other words, I know when I preach on any given weekend that most of the people I speak to are *not going to come* to the mission.

That was tremendously hard for me at first. I can remember feeling angry because I felt more people should have come on the first night of the mission. This has been part of the crucifixion of my flesh. I am being purified of being in control. My motivation for preaching missions has been sifted. My attitude has been checked. Now, I have two purposes for my weekend homily. 1) I try to get as many people as I can to attend the mission, and 2) I minister the best I can to the *people who are there* that weekend, knowing that I only have one crack at them because most of them will not be back. I am OK with that. It is not all about me. I have the ability to bounce back and be resilient in Christ. God has used my ministry to put me to death and raise me up again. God is using your circumstances to do the same.

One story that helps me as a preacher illustrates that even Jesus had to deal with low percentages. Remember the story of the ten lepers who were healed? (Luke 17:11-19) Jesus healed ten lepers by speaking to them and they all went to the priests to verify the cleansing. One of them, and a Samaritan on top of it (at odds with the Jews) came back praising God and giving thanks to Jesus. Jesus said, "Were not ten cleansed? Where are the other nine?" I often think of how hurt Jesus must have been at that. Only one came back. As I talk to ministers and fellow priests around the country, one thing that hurts them is how few people come to daily Mass or weekend services. A minister can have the tendency to take it personally and blame and beat him or herself up. Even Jesus himself only had ten percent come back! Few appreciated what they had. I have come to understand that there will always be an *anawim* (a small remnant) who will come. It's just the way it is. I have come to accept this.

THE TRAVAILS OF TRAVEL

I am not complaining here, but there is a tremendous loss of control doing what I do. Once I leave home and get to the airport, everything is out of my hands. Since I am a Type A personality, I try to do things excellently and love to be in control. Waiting in lines at the airports and checking baggage teaches me to how to wait. Flying means a loss of control for me. (Have you flown lately?) There have been times when I land and get my baggage, and still no one has identified himself as the person picking me up. I feel so helpless and out of control in those moments as I wait.

Once I get to the rectory, I am living in someone else's home for the week. I do not have control over the food situation (and I love to eat!) Most of my missions are east of California and I have to adjust to losing two or three hours because of the time zone variances (ever try preaching at 5 a.m.?) I have to adapt to the bed which may be soft, the pillow which may be hard, the air conditioning which may be too cold or the heat which may be too hot. I am usually given the room by the kitchen, furnace, air conditioning units, TV or street traffic. It tends to be noisy. (I am very sensitive to noise!) Every sense is assaulted. Often the dust from long unused pillows clogs my breathing. Trying to find where everything is in the morning to get breakfast is a challenge. I am meeting lots of different people at the same time. The sound systems never seem to work perfectly and that is how I make my living! Some churches are in the round. Others are narrow and long. Some have people sitting behind me (which I hate), others have pillars in front of me. Again, I am not complaining, this is my call, and I've embraced it, but I am saying that life takes flexibility, adaptability, and resilience no matter what you do!

Initially, in every new situation I go into, I have the feeling of being stripped. I am on the road and in front of a new group of people. I have learned to focus on the positive and not concentrate on the negative. We all have difficult situations and people in our life. God is using them to teach us so that we can grow. Sanctification does not come in a vacuum or just on a mountain top somewhere; rather, it comes through the real everyday stuff of our lives.

I realize most of you aren't missionaries. I tell you my experiences so that you will think of your own. Everyone has a different flavor of difficulties. Perhaps you don't like your wife's perfume. Possibly her cooking upsets you. Maybe you don't like the fact that your husband watches too much sports on TV or doesn't take you dancing. You've tried to change these situations and nothing seems to work. Reality that is out of control in our life is the "stuff" that God uses to bring *us under control*.

The bottom line is that God is there to help you in every situation and challenge you may have in your life. I have learned a lot of trust, flexibility and resilience as a result of what God is doing in my life. I have learned to lean on and depend on Jesus ever more radically and fully. Strangely, when I am stripped I discover union with Jesus by identifying with his sufferings.

Jesus handled his problems beautifully. He did not let people, places, and events determine his attitude. Rather, he lived passionately as he put his trust in God, learned, grew and kept pressing on. He made great choices with his life. Whatever situation God has you in, never give up. In Christ you can bounce back day by day. (Through him, with him, and in him!) Learn to be adaptable and flexible. Focus on the positive. You can do it! Rely on Christ ever more fully. Choose life and live. God is after your attitude! Attitude may not be everything, but it is a lot!

† Chapter 8 †

I CAN DO ALL THINGS
(Philippians 4:13)

On my pilgrimage to Israel, Greece and Rome in 1999, one of the places we journeyed to was Philippi in northern Greece. We got to see the archeological ruins of the prison Paul was kept in. Prisons at the time of Paul the apostle were cold, dark, dingy and lonely. Acts 16:25-34 tells us the story of what happened in that prison. "About midnight Paul and Silas were praying and singing hymns to God, and the prisoners were listening to them . . ."

This story tells me a lot about Paul's attitude and his resilience. He was singing in prison! In the middle of the night! No matter what "prison" you may feel you are in, sing and pray and watch earthquakes happen. The greatest earthquake may not have been terrestrial. The most profound shaking happened to those listening to Paul and Silas singing. The jailer himself came over to Paul and said, "What must I do to be saved?" They wanted what Paul had. His positive, joyful attitude in the midst of his situation "released" the one guarding him! In verse 16:34, we read that then the jailer "rejoiced with all his household." Positive attitudes are catchy.

Later on Paul would write to his community at Philippi, "Not that I complain of want; for I have *learned,* in whatever state I am, to be *content*. I know how to be abased, and I know how to abound; in any and all circumstances I have learned the secret of facing plenty and hunger, abundance and want. *I can do all things in Christ who strengthens me.*" (Philippians 4:11-13) Notice, instead of constantly saying "I can't do it," Paul said, "I *can* do it." He learned this truth. He found the secret. He was able to be content *in Christ*.

I have struggled for many years with doubts about myself and my abilities. Often I will think "I can't do it." This is something that has troubled me since my childhood. When I was twelve years old, I was on the little league baseball team in Agawam, Massachusetts where I grew up. Actually, it was our church league and behind our church we had a great baseball diamond with lights and a state of the art scoreboard.

I have always been good at sports and baseball was my favorite sport growing up. I had good eye/hand coordination and could hit the ball well. Also, because I was fleet of foot, I was placed in center field to cover more ground. I did very well that year and helped our team win many games.

Every year on July 4th, we had the midsummer classic, the All Star game. Two players were chosen from every team to represent each team in the game. Lo and behold I was chosen from our team along with a teammate. Now, I had been to these All Star games in the past as a spectator. Fans would pack the stands to watch the game. Teammates, relatives, peers and others would all be there. People literally lined the outfield fence in order to see. It was the game of the season!

I remember the day of the game came and it was a beautiful sunny day. There were a few puffy clouds, the smell of popcorn was in the air and everything you needed for a ball game was there. Only one thing was missing. The centerfielder for our team wasn't there. You see, during the game, I was at home in bed with a stomach ache watching a movie. The movie I was watching wasn't on TV. Rather, the movie I was watching was in my head and it kept playing like a rerun over and over.

Here's what I saw: It's the bottom of the ninth inning. There are two out. We are ahead by one run. They have the bases loaded. All we have to do is get one more out and we win the game. I'm out there in center field thinking to myself, "Don't hit it to me. Please! Don't hit it to me," and trying to look calm. Suddenly, there's the pitch and the crack of the bat can be heard as a high arching fly ball is launched straight to centerfield. There is a hush over the crowd as the ball begins to come down. If I catch it we win, if I miss it, disaster. I see myself circling under the ball, opening my glove and watching with horror as the ball hits the heel of my glove and pops out. I drop it.

I saw this over and over again, so often that my anxiety made my stomach churn and I didn't go to the game. You see, my coach thought I could do it, my teammates voted me in, my parents believed in me, but deep down, I didn't think I could do it. In my imagination, I was saying to myself over and over again, "I can't do it." I hated myself for not having the courage to at least try.

THROUGH HIM, WITH HIM AND IN HIM

As you know, now I preach to more people at most Masses than ever would have been at that game. I travel around the country sharing the Good News with crowds that have surpassed 1,500 at times. I have learned a secret, too. I can do all things **in Christ** who strengthens me. This secret was learned and it took time. As I gave my life to Jesus more and more, he gave me the courage to try things and to break the self-imposed boundaries in my life. I find new strength that certainly I do not have in and of myself. I am not writing about self-confidence here; rather, I am proclaiming God-confidence.

Every year I get away for a week on my own and take a retreat. I treasure this time alone with God and his Word and look forward to how the Lord will speak to me during this time. One year I went to a Franciscan retreat center located at the entrance of Sequoia National Park in California. It is about 1,000 feet in altitude at the foot of the Sierras. I spent a good deal of time each day simply staring at the mountains in silence. It is amazing how they speak to you when you contemplate them. At night, because we were far from bright lights, the stars would shine brightly. I could actually see the cloud of the Milky Way galaxy overhead. I would wake up in the middle of the night and go out and gaze as my mouth dropped open. It was so quiet.

I sensed God saying to me that the eternal power and might that formed those mountains and hung those stars is available to me. It took millions of years and a lot of patience and grace to form creation. God's magnificence and glory live in us and can be released to help us. One of the words in the Greek for power is *dunamis*. I like to say that it is God's "can do power." We get the word dynamite from this. God's power is strength and might to make us able. God has not anointed us for easy things, but to be able to do what he has called us to do.

THE IMMEASURABLE GREATNESS OF HIS POWER (Ephesians 1:19)

This inner strength, confidence, power, energy, enthusiasm and passion to live is available to you. Often when a married person comes to confession, after they confess, I will lay hands on his or her head and say, "God is strengthening you and giving you power to live your vocation well." In other words, there is might, married people, to raise your children, forgive and keep pressing on. There is strength, students, to accomplish your work in school and follow your dreams. There is grace, single people, to deal with loneliness and trials. There is an anointing, priests and those called to serve, to show forth Christ by your words and life. There is power, follower of Christ, to pray, overcome temptation and live passionately!

In 1983, the year before I joined the Passionists, I served as a youth minister in the city of St. Louis, Missouri. My ministry there was twofold. First of all, I was responsible for initiating and maintaining a youth group in the local parish. I loved doing this and while the numbers weren't large, the young people who came each week were great kids. I found this ministry very satisfying and rewarding.

The second part of my ministry was the hard part. I was a "prefect" in a college preparatory high school called Chaminade. This meant that I lived in a dormitory with about one hundred teenage high school boys. My task was to make sure they got off to school on time, did their homework, got to bed on time, and other parental type duties.

My bedroom was actually below ground level. If I looked out of my bedroom window, I saw the grass at eye level. High schoolers' rooms surrounded me. The noise was incredible, especially in the morning when I was "off" and free to sleep in. Since I have a rather gentle personality, I wasn't mean and harsh and tried to be friends with the boys. I think they took advantage of that on occasion. I struggled with being their friend and somehow being their disciplinarian. It was hard for me to raise my voice and make them do things like their homework. When could I let things slide and when did I have to lower the boom? Many of you who are reading this book who are parents know the symptoms. Parenting is difficult and there aren't many manuals out there about how to do it. Much of it is trial and error and mistakes are made.

There were many frustrating moments and times of self doubt for me in that year. It was difficult. I struggled. It was hard. One day as I was reading the Bible, I came upon Philippians 4:13, "I can do all things in Christ who strengthens me." When I read that I was inspired to think that the "all things" the Bible talked about meant my situation, too. I sensed God encouraging me and strengthening me through his word to this task that he called me to.

I never forgot that moment of inspiration. After I read the Bible that day, I took a piece of paper and a magic marker and wrote out Philippians 4:13 on the paper. I cut off that portion of the paper and actually taped it to the mirror where I shaved in the morning. Every morning when I got up, first thing in the morning, as my doubts were screaming, "What disaster is going to happen today?" I would go in the bathroom and look at that quote, "I can do all things in Christ who strengthens me." I would remember that it was not *me* doing the things I was called to do that particular day. It was Christ in me doing them. Plus, I *was able* in Christ to do them! I will never forget how that one verse taped to my mirror encouraged me and gave me the grace to be victorious and live passionately during a very difficult year in my life.

STABILITY IN THE STORM

One of our Mass sites on the May 1999 pilgrimage was the Catacomb of St. Calistius in Rome. The Catacombs, as you know, were the underground tunnels where Christians would gather to celebrate Eucharist and to pray during the persecution. Many Christians were also buried there and the tombs of these popes and saints were venerated. Until Constantine made Christianity the official state religion in Rome in the 300's, it was often a religion on the run and many courageous people were martyred by the Roman government for their faith.

Etched into one of the walls of this catacomb is one of the earliest Christian symbols known. It is an anchor with the cross on the top of the anchor. The biblical verse corresponding to this is Hebrews 6:19. "We have this hope (of eternal life in Jesus) as a sure and steadfast *anchor of the soul*, a hope that enters into the inner shrine behind the curtain."

When a storm is approaching, the captain of a ship will take the boat out of dock and moor it in the harbor. The heavy anchor will stabilize the ship when the wind and waves buffet the boat. When it is dragged, the two sharp ends of the anchor will grab hold of the mud and sand below and stabilize the ship.

This symbolizes what Jesus is for the believer. When storms of health problems blow into our lives, it is Jesus who holds us fast. When the hurricane of the death of a loved one ravages our boat, it is Jesus who stabilizes us and helps us to cope. When the rain of trials and tribulations tries to drag us around aimlessly, the anchor that is Jesus secures us and keeps us. Jesus is our anchor and our strength. No matter the wind, waves, trials or difficulties, Jesus keeps us steadfast and firm!

Many people in the world today have boats without anchors. They are tossed about by every wind and doctrine that comes down the pike. Families are ruptured because they have no stability. Some people flit around to different churches and religions because they have no anchor. Others turn to alcohol, drugs, gambling, TV and other forms of escapism to cope with the sufferings of life because they don't know Jesus. Wise is the person who has an anchor in his or her life to face the inevitable storms that will come. Jesus will anchor you through any storm you may encounter, even death! Bind yourself to this anchor as tightly as possible now, before the storm hits. Then, when the winds blow, you will not be shipwrecked.

9
OCEAN OF LOVE
"The Passion of Jesus is a sea of sorrows but it is also an ocean of love."
(St. Paul of the Cross)

HOLY, HOLY, HOLY IS THE LORD
(Isaiah 6:3)

I have touched on the subject of sanctification and would like to explain this further. Sanctification is the process, the journey of life that makes us holy. Our call to holiness is found everywhere in the Bible. One instance is 1 Peter 1:15-16. "As God who called you is holy, be holy yourselves in all your conduct; since it is written, 'You shall be holy for I am holy.'" We are to be holy because that is the way God is. We are to become like God, like Christ.

It was once thought that holiness was the job of priests and religious and that lay people were somehow exempt from this. Vatican II put that notion to death when it proclaimed that there is a **"universal"** call to holiness. In the Vatican II document, *Lumen Gentium* #39, we read, "Therefore, all in the Church, whether they belong to the hierarchy or are cared for by it, are called to holiness." In other words, **all** are called to be holy. Holiness can be found in a monastery, yes, but holiness can and should be manifested in every vocation. Married people, single people and religious all have the call to holiness.

Holiness basically means to be separated. Separated from what? From sin and from evil. Separated for what? For God alone. God is totally other. God is separated from anything that is vile or unclean. God does not sin and is perfect in love. I wish I could put into words the awesome, powerful, glorious, electric presence of God that I experienced at my conversion. God is holy in that there is none like him. God is light and there is no darkness, no evil, no hint of anything unloving or unjust in God.

A very interesting reality occurs when people encounter God. There is an intense feeling of unworthiness. I love this story from the prophet Isaiah.

> In the year the King Uzziah died *I saw the Lord* sitting upon a throne, high and lifted up; and his train filled the temple . . . The angels called one to another and said: "Holy, holy, holy is the Lord of hosts; the whole earth is full of his glory." And I said: "Woe is me! For I am lost; for I am a man of unclean lips, and I dwell in the midst of a people of unclean lips; for my eyes have seen the King, the Lord of hosts!" Then an angel touched my mouth (with the burning coal from the altar) and said: "Behold this has touched your lips; your guilt is taken away, and your sin forgiven." And I heard the voice of the Lord saying, "Whom shall I send, and who will go for us?" Then I said, "Here am I! Send me." And God said, "Go." (Isaiah 6:1-8)

Isaiah the prophet had a majestic vision of the Lord. He was privileged to be taken to the Lord and shown God's glory. Notice what it was the angels were chanting: "Holy, holy, holy." They were proclaiming God's complete separation from anything evil and God's uniqueness of being. When I preside at the Eucharist, I always try to slow down and have a sense of awe when we say or sing these words at Mass, "Holy, holy, holy, Lord God of power and might, heaven and earth are full of your glory!" Then if I pray Eucharistic Prayer II, I continue by praying, "Lord you are holy indeed, the fountain of all holiness. Let your Holy Spirit come down upon these gifts to make them holy . . ."

The Lord has prompted me to write my second book about the Holy Spirit. I will write more then, but now, I simply want you to notice who the Spirit of God is: **Holy**, the Holy Spirit. The book of Wisdom has a lot to say about God's Spirit. "For a holy and disciplined spirit will flee from deceit and rise and depart from foolish thoughts and be ashamed at the approach of unrighteousness." (Wisdom 1:5) In other words, holiness and deceit do not go together. When listing the qualities of wisdom, the author of the Book of Wisdom notes that "She is a breath of the power of God and a pure emanation of the glory of the Almighty; therefore *nothing defiled gains entrance into her.*" (Wisdom 7:25)

LORD, I AM NOT WORTHY . . .
(Matthew 9:8)

Whenever a person in the Bible has an authentic encounter with God, unworthiness is experienced. We hear Isaiah say, "Woe is me!" (Isaiah 6:5) He had a profound sense of his sinfulness (especially of the mouth) and God's purity.

Interestingly, Peter also had this experience at the Sea of Galilee. When Jesus told him to put out into the deep for a catch, Peter obeyed. When he caught a great number of fish, suddenly Peter came to a deep realization of just who Jesus of Nazareth was. He began by calling Jesus Master (Luke 5:5), then progressed to call him Lord.

(Luke 5:8). He saw the purity and integrity of this carpenter from Galilee and he realized that Jesus was more than just a carpenter, teacher or master. He was the Lord. With this encounter came the sense of unworthiness. "But when Simon Peter saw the catch, he fell down at Jesus' knees, saying, 'Depart from me, for I am a sinful man, O Lord'" (Luke 5:8)

Moses also had this experience when he encountered the Holy at the burning bush. He realized that he was on "holy ground" and then Moses hid his face and was afraid to look at God. This "fear," the fear of the Lord, (one of the seven gifts of the Holy Spirit–Isaiah 11:2-3) is a profound sense of the presence of God. Certainly it is reverence for God's manifest presence and includes the desire not to offend; but also, it is a deep sense of our unworthiness and sinfulness and God's absolute purity and majesty. Make no mistake about it, God is holy (separated from evil) and if we are to stand in God's presence, we must be purified.

The pendulum has swung in Church preaching and teaching today. In the 1940's and 50's there was a tremendous emphasis on "hellfire and brimstone" preaching. This type of preaching was especially popular during parish missions. The goal was to scare people half to death. Today, and rightly so, the emphasis is on God's love. God is in love with us. That is what this book is all about. But I think there needs to be balanced teaching. I do no one a favor unless I proclaim one of the basic messages of the Gospel, repentance from sin.

What so often happens is that people hear about God being love and make God out to be anything they want God to be. Sometimes, because God is so loving and forgiving, people will presume God's mercy. Absolutely, God is love, but God's mercy is not to be presumed. God's love is an aspect of God's holiness, God's otherness. God is awesome, powerful, magnificent and majestic. God is separated from evil. Ask the Holy Spirit for the gift of the fear of the Lord. You will be given authentic experiences of God that will humble you and leave you in awe. Understanding will come with experience. When the student is ready, the teacher will come.

BE STILL AND KNOW
(Psalm 46:10)

One of my favorite stories on the subject of prayer in the Bible, and one I like to preach about, comes from 1 Kings 19:9-13. "Elijah came to a cave (on Mt. Horeb) and the word of the Lord came to him and said, 'Go forth, and stand upon the mount before the Lord.' And behold, the Lord passed by, and a great and strong wind rent the mountains, and broke in pieces the rocks before the Lord, but the Lord was *not* in the wind; and after the wind an earthquake, but the Lord was *not* in the earthquake; and after the earthquake a fire, but the Lord was *not* in the fire; and after the fire a *still small voice*. And when Elijah heard it, he wrapped his face in his mantle and went out and stood at the entrance of the cave."

God is awesome and majestic, true, but a major aspect of his holiness is what I call God's *tenderness*. There is something very delicate and even fragile about our God. Elijah encountered God not so much in the wind, earthquake and fire but in the stillness of a whisper. Whispers tickle. Whispers are intriguing. Whispers make us listen more closely. The sound of a lover whispering, "I love you" shouts!

The Christmas story speaks volumes to me about the humility and even vulnerability of our God. The messiah was born, not in a castle, but in a cave to poor parents. The shepherds and Magi looked upon the face of a vulnerable little baby. To me, the Christmas story preaches about the holiness of God. God's holiness is demonstrated in power, yes, but also in humility, tenderness, graciousness and love. God is a little baby being born. Can you appreciate such holiness?

I have always loved cats. Our family had them growing up. One place I always encounter the holiness of God is in a kitten. Have you ever looked at a one week old kitten? They are so frail, soft and needy. They shake and their eyes are so cute and they meow daintily. They are the picture of innocence and gentleness. Whenever I see a kitten, I think of God. The God who spoke the universe into being with a word also created the kitten. That's why violence is such a sin against holiness. It is not God's nature. God's heart is very innocent and gentle. Remember Jesus' words, "Learn from me, for I am gentle and meek of heart." (Matthew 11:29)

We can be so violent and fast paced in our thinking and acting. It is easy to be harsh and critical toward others and ourselves. When we are like this, we lose a major sense of God. It is no surprise that two of the "fruits" of the Holy Spirit are kindness and gentleness. (Galatians 5:22-23) It is simply who God is. Passionate living involves being gentle toward ourselves and others.

One of the major thrusts of most retreats and missions I've given and attended is the theme, "slow down." What that phrase means is to slow down our thoughts and body and relax. Be kind to yourself and others in your thinking. There is no reason to be frantic. Don't be in a hurry. Notice things and savor the moment. I invite you to do that right now. Relax. Slow down. I pray that this book will be a catalyst for helping you to enter the presence of God.

At our residence in Sacramento we have a fireplace. In the winter I love to stand by the warmth of the fireplace and watch the flames leap up from the logs. There is something very hypnotizing about a fire. It relaxes me and mellows my thought process. I begin to think of God and become less violent and hurried in my thinking. I reflect on my life and what God is doing in me. I sense the gentleness and holiness of God.

HOW SWEET IS YOUR LOVE
(Song of Songs 4:10)

When it comes to trying to "capture" God's holiness, words fail. I love the creativity and inspiration of musicians who create gentle songs with acoustic guitar, flute, saxophone, harp and piano. As musicians sing about God's tender love and mercy, I am ushered into God's holy presence. Think of some of your favorite slow songs about God. Don't they draw you into a sense of the holy? Don't they in some way inspire you about the graciousness and softness of our God? I always feel that music is a major part of the experience of a mission. There are times when the music of a well done solo will capture what words cannot preach. It stills us and creates an openness through which God can move and bless people.

God is there in stillness and gentleness. God's tenderness, stillness and love is holy. Psalm 46:10 invites us to "Be still and know that I am God." In addition to music, the quiet of meditation and contemplation helps us to appreciate and know the gentleness as well as the majesty of God's holiness.

10
TRANSFORMED IN GOD

"As you are crucified with Christ, you become more and more transformed in God through faith and love." (St. Paul of the Cross)

DON'T BE CONFORMED, BE TRANSFORMED
(Romans 12:2)

A person who is holy is consecrated in body, mind, will and emotions away from sin toward God. To be holy is to give yourself to God. I always say that to be holy is to be "wholly" given to the Lord. The reality is that most of the time we are *partly* given to God. Our life journey is to become set apart more and more. We are called to be special vessels for God's use and to be set apart for God and God alone. (2 Timothy 2:20-22)

There is a Trappist (Cistercian) abbey in Kentucky called Gethsemane. I occasionally like to spend time with the Trappists because of their tradition of prayer and simplicity. This community is cloistered and after a man joins, he almost never leaves the grounds of the abbey. These men pray many times a day and live a very rigorous life of prayer, work and penance. They live with the same people day after day after day. They wake up in the same place day after day after day. I like to say that they "play for keeps."

I was walking up the stairs at the abbey in Gethsemane one Sunday. Just before I entered the church I looked to my right and saw something striking etched in concrete. There were two words: "God alone." That is the notion of holiness.

Not that you have to live in a monastery, but that your entire life is committed to and consecrated to God alone. This can happen in any walk of life, but it must happen.

"I appeal to you therefore, brothers and sisters, by the mercies of God, to present your bodies (entire selves) as a living sacrifice holy and acceptable to God, which is your spiritual worship. Do not be conformed to this world but be transformed by the renewal of your mind, that you may prove what is the will of God, what is good and acceptable and perfect." (Romans 12:1-2)

When you think about it, you will realize that besides our physical body and spirit, we are basically comprised of a mind (thoughts), emotions (feelings), and a will (decisions). I want, I think and I feel. I want, I think and I feel. In fact I studied the beautiful discipline of philosophy for a year before I entered the Passionists and remember studying the famous philosopher, Descartes, who said, "I think therefore I am." For him the proof of our being is the fact that we think. I once saw a sign on a golf bag of a person with a sense of humor. The sign said, "I golf, therefore I swear . . ." I've met a lot of people on the course with that philosophy, that's for sure.

Throughout our lives we are conformed to this world. We listen to what people say. We think like others think. We watch our parents. We imitate our friends. We allow TV and books and the values of other people to permeate our being. From birth until the day we die we are constantly bombarded with this world's philosophy. Whether we recognize it or not, we conform.

Romans 12 tells us that because we have been conformed to values and ways opposite to God's, we must now be transformed. Transformation for me is one of the most beautiful words in the Bible. You can be transformed! Sanctification is the process of being transformed. The place where this happens is in the mind (Romans 12:2), the emotions, and the will.

THE KINGDOM OF GOD IS AT HAND; REPENT (Mark 1:15)

First of all, our thoughts must change. The word repentance in the Bible comes from the Greek word *metanoia* which means "change your mind." A penny for your thoughts . . . is your mind helping you or hurting you? Worldly thoughts are lustful, negative, anxious, envious, greedy, cynical and selfish. Your mind can be renewed through the events of your lives and the grace of God. A holy person has his or her mind consecrated to God. She lives in trust and peace.

Secondly, our emotions must change. Many people are up when their circumstances are up and down when their circumstances are down. I call this roller coaster Christianity. Transformation does not mean that you don't have emotions, rather it means that you are able to manage your emotions and you have greater stability and balance in your life.

Thirdly, our wills must be transformed. Many times our decisions are *me* oriented. What about me? What about me? What about me? A holy person begins to desire what God wants over self and begins to think of the needs of others. Rather than selfishness, self*less*ness ensues. A person who has been sanctified is a lover. The call to holiness is also a call to discipline the will. That is why the fruit of self-control is so important.

I have discovered that separation to God (holiness) is a matter of degree. We are all at different points on the holiness scale. One major way to tell how dedicated you are to God is to notice your body. For example, what about your eyes? Do you look at TV shows that are ungodly? If you are watching soap operas and other worldly shows, that is an indication that you are carnal. In fact, I call those remote channel changers "moral indicators." When you think about it, they indicate exactly where you are spiritually. I know people who put a sign up on their TV set. It says, "Would Jesus watch this show with you?" I fly through airports quite a bit and will stop in magazine stores. It is amazing what they put on the covers of magazines today. I find myself having to avert my eyes often. The desire to linger on inappropriate magazines is an indication of just how set apart to God your eyes are. (Matthew 6:22-23)

YOU WILL EAT YOUR OWN WORDS

What about your mouth? I love to play golf and when I am at home I will go out to the course in my shorts and golf shirt looking like anyone else. The starter will usually join me up with two or three other guys. In the beginning, they may hit the ball well, then the true game emerges. People start slicing it into the woods, or hooking it into the water. I've seen clubs fly and people kick bags. People call themselves "Dummy" and many swear. After a bad shot I will inevitably hear, "Jesus!" this, and "Jesus!" that; "G.D.!" this and "G.D.!" that. I'll be thinking, "This guy prays more than I do!" Actually the name of God is used more on a golf course on Monday than it is in church on Sunday. (Sometimes by the same people going to church on Sunday!)

Then after nine holes or so, we'll all be standing up on the teebox. We've already talked about the weather and the sports teams, and now the conversation is going to get a little deeper. Inevitably one of the guys in the foursome will ask, "Hey Cedric, what do you do for a living?" Then I will swallow, look them in the eyes and reply, "I'm a Catholic priest!" You can always tell the Catholics in the foursome. They are the ones who turn red because of their swearing!

If a person is embarrassed because of swearing in front of a Catholic priest, what will it be like when they stand before the Almighty whose name they were taking in vain? Words are **indications** of where you are on the holiness scale. Jesus made a stunning, sobering statement in Matthew 12:37, "By your words you will be justified and by your words you will be condemned."

Gossip, negativity, murmuring, complaining, swearing, off color jokes and lying are serious matters. One of the first things God called me to change in myself was the way I spoke. I was delivered from a bad habit of swearing. It takes our decision and God's grace to overcome it. Be aware of what you are saying. Is your mouth saved?

I am aware that God has been dealing with me about my mouth for some time. I consciously try to discipline myself to be quiet especially when gossip is being thrown around the supper table. God will let you get by with slander for a while, then he will have enough and start "dealing" with you. What I mean by this is that God is at work in us and uses life's circumstances to touch our experience.

I can remember one incident recently when I was talking about someone behind his back. I knew I shouldn't be doing this, but did it anyway. (This is carnality!) Afterwards I looked for something to eat and decided to have some chicken noodle soup. I brought it to a boil and dished some out in the bowl and sat down to eat. It was very hot and as I ate it, I knew I was burning my tongue. I tried to be careful, but couldn't avoid getting burnt. I hate that feeling when my taste buds get scorched. Afterwards, I thought, "This feels weird, I have to preach tomorrow and I feel like I can't even talk well because my tongue is seared."

Then it dawned on me. I had been gossiping and using my tongue for evil. Ordinarily I would think, "It was because of the soup." But, looking a little more deeply, I knew instinctively that it was God dealing with me. Every time I felt my tongue when I talked or ate, I thought, "This is from God." The Bible talks about chastisement in many places. Hebrews 12:10 says, "God disciplines us for our good, that we may share his holiness." This is one little example of the innumerable ways that God uses the events of our lives to speak to us and correct us. Someone gave me a card with a statement on it recently. The card said, "May the words that I speak today be sweet–for tomorrow I may have to eat them." I learned about that first hand. There are books out called "Chicken Soup for the Soul." Well, I learned that God also gives us chicken soup for the mouth!

Are you taking care of your body? It is clear that we are the temple of God. Are you behaving immorally? Do you exercise, eat well, rest enough, go to the doctor once in a while? Do you take drugs, smoke or drink too much? The bottom line is this: "You are not your own; you were bought with a price. So glorify God in your body." (1 Corinthians 6:19-20) The way you treat your own body(which is a gift) is an indication of your separation unto God.

Separation unto God means that you give God your time. All of us, no matter how busy we are, have free time. What do you do with your leisure time? Do you include God in it? Yes, it is good and okay to rest and watch some TV and recreate, but we need to have balance in this area. Too much honey makes one sick! (Proverbs 25:16)

SURFING U.S.A.

Every once in a while I am able to go to Florida to visit Mom and Dad. When I am there I play golf, hit the beach, visit with my parents and rest. After I've done all that, I like to sit down and watch some TV. I love "surfing," channel surfing, that is. It is fun to use the remote to see what's on.

My parents have one of the huge big screen TV's in their living room. They have cable and get a lot of channels. After I've hit the beach and played golf, I'll come into their house, grab the remote, and settle into the chair. Interesting thing about these easy chairs, it is like they have "fingers" that reach out and grab you and pull you into the chair . . . so comfortable!

I've noticed that the local news begins in Florida at 5 p.m. Then, the local news continues at 5:30 p.m. Then the local news continues at 6 p.m. Then, after one and a half hours of knowing about every evil deed done in the central Florida area, the national news comes on at 6:30 p.m. Then, of course, there is Jeopardy, Wheel of Fortune, Seinfeld, Home Improvement, Who Wants to be a Millionaire?, Monday Night Football . . . et cetera! Before I know it I've spent five hours in front of the TV and haven't moved except to go to the fridge to get a bite to eat. It's easy to get sucked in!

Now, I'm not saying that you shouldn't watch TV. There is a lot of excellent programming on television. It is understandable that a person would want to come home and watch some news and a few other things. But what starts to happen is that people get hooked and trapped in a TV stronghold. I read an article in the U.S.A. Today newspaper some time back that said the average American watches TV for four hours per day. I don't know about you, but I think four hours a day is too much! Never mind what is *on* some of those programs. Jesus taught, "Where your treasure is, there will your heart be also." (Matthew 6:19) Where is your treasure? Where are you spending your time? Where is your heart?

Whenever I spend too long watching the TV, my body starts to tell me. My back starts to ache, I feel lethargic and passive and sometimes I start to get a headache. Once in a while I'll tune into those daytime talk shows and as I watch, I notice my emotions start to change. It is easy to be influenced by what's on and feel despair. I don't know where they get the people who are on those shows! I know instinctively that it is time to move and get away from that thing. You may disagree with me on this point, but I know that by simply by turning off the TV, people can develop their relationship with God by reading, praying or spending more quality time with their family. An addiction is anything you surrender to. If you are caught in TV addiction, pray for deliverance. God will help you.

THE BIBLE IS A BOOK OF RELATIONSHIPS

One other area relating to holiness is relationships. I believe that if you pray for believing friends, God will favor you with friends who have faith. I have met people all over this country who are good, honest, loving people. I keep in touch with many of them. They are a gift to me from God.

Other relationships can pull you away from God. Many people will develop relationships with people because of the way that they seem. They seem to be nice and considerate. Yet, when you look beyond the surface, that person's desires and values may not be godly. Many people are lonely and want a spouse so badly that impatience takes over and they do not wait. Broken marriages can ensue. Friendships can come to a dead end. At some point one person in the relationship realizes that his or her values are very different from the other's. People who are not Christlike can actually have a bad effect on a Christian. That is why we are warned to choose carefully the people we spend time with.

> What has a believer in common with an unbeliever? What agreement has the temple of God with idols? For we are the temple of the living God; as God said, I will live in them and move among them and I will be their God, and they shall be my people. Therefore come out from them and **be separate from them**, says the Lord, and touch nothing unclean; then I will welcome you, and I will be a father to you and you shall be my sons and daughters, says the Lord Almighty.
> (2 Corinthians 6:15-18)

This may seem a bit harsh. Obviously Jesus dined with sinners and people who did not know God. I am not saying stay away from people; however, we must use wisdom in choosing our friends and partners. They will influence us whether we know it or not. I have learned through experience in my life that some people are simply not good for me. I've learned not to get entangled with people who don't share similar values. (2 Timothy 2:4) I try to choose my friends very carefully.

If you are in a marriage and you are not getting along with your spouse or they do not support you in your Christian faith, please understand that I am not saying to leave them. I hear from spouses (women and men) that their partner is not at the same level spiritually as they are. This causes great distress and is a great suffering. I don't believe God is calling you to leave them: the commitment has already been made. If you stay dedicated to your commitment before God, God will honor that fidelity. You probably won't be able to change your spouse, but God will change *you*! Along with God changing you through your spouse, God may just change your partner also in *God's* timing and *God's* ways, so don't give up!

YOU SHALL LOVE
(Mark 12:28)

The idea of holiness can be summed up with this story from the Gospel of Mark.

> A scribe came up to Jesus and questioned him, "Which commandment is the first of all?" Jesus answered, "The first is, 'Hear, O Israel: The Lord our God, the Lord is one; and you shall love the Lord your God with all your heart, and

with all your soul and with all your mind and with all your strength.' The second is this, 'You shall love your neighbor as yourself.' There is no other commandment greater than these."
(Mark 12:28-31)

Do you love God? God has called us into a love relationship. I remember when I first started dating. I noticed that there are stages in a relationship. First you meet someone, then you feel attracted toward them, then you begin to get to know them, like them, become infatuated with them, and somewhere down the line you actually **fall in love** with that person. When that happens, there is an exclusivity in the relationship. This can be symbolized by the wearing of an engagement ring or some article of clothing that shows the dedication you have toward the other person.

When you fall in love there is a bonding, an emotional connectedness and a deep affection for the other person. You want to spend time with them. There is a lot of energy, creativity, enthusiasm, and communication. You have that person on your mind quite a bit and you look forward to being with that person. Psychologists tell us that love is more than a feeling, it is a decision. If you are truly in love with God, you will constantly make the decision to do what is pleasing to him.

I believe when Jesus talked about loving God with all your heart, soul, mind and strength, he was actually speaking about being "in love" with God. A love relationship with God can be highly passionate, emotional and intimate. Jesus was saying that God has an exclusive claim on your thoughts, feelings, will, time and energy. Lovers reveal aspects of their deepest selves to the other. God will reveal aspects of himself to you that you couldn't learn otherwise. You will **know** God in a personal way. Flowing from this intimacy will come a desire to be set apart for God completely.

DO AS I HAVE DONE TO YOU
(John 13:15)

A major part of holiness is the willingness to love and to serve others. That is the second part of the love command (love God, and love others). The basic thrust I had toward other people all came as a result of my loving God. If you want to truly love God (and this is a major part of holiness) you must be a servant and love others.

When I went to college I began by majoring in business. I wasn't sure exactly what I wanted to do, but I knew that I wanted to make a lot of money. That was my goal. It seemed like the American dream was to go to school, get educated, and the system would reward you with a good job and prosperity. I was looking for that. I wanted to live comfortably, settle down, get married, and be happy. (I am not saying that you cannot be a person with a job in business and be holy. I have met many business men and women of integrity who are committed to Jesus Christ. I was invited to examine my motives, however.)

In the midst of this overriding goal for my life, I invited Jesus in to be Lord of my life. I experienced God. In time, I began to fall in love with God and to yield to God more and more of my mind, heart, soul and strength. I noticed in time that my motivations began to change. I went from desiring money to desiring to help people. I began to become aware of the tremendous needs people have. As God took over more and more, I went from selfishness to selflessness.

There was a lot of confusion for me in those years of college. Many young people struggle with what they are about and who they are. I began to lose my motivation for studying business and my grades began to slip. My heart wasn't in it any longer. I had worked so hard the first two years in college and had made great grades. In my third year, I even flunked my accounting course. I was horrified, but it indicated where I was in my heart. My heart was no longer toward money. I knew that I wanted to be involved with people.

At the conclusion of my third year, I made a radical change in my courses. I made the decision to change my major to social work. That meant that I would end up losing a year's worth of credits. Many of the credits I had earned in business could not be applied toward the degree in community services. I had to go to college for an extra year. That was a tough pill to swallow, but there was no other choice for me. I simply wasn't motivated to study anything having to do with finances.

My grades improved drastically the next two years. I was working toward a goal that, for me, was Christlike. I was motivated to study. I was spending my time and life toward a goal that had significance and meaning. I was working toward a life of serving people. At the time I had little idea that I would be called to the priesthood. God took me forward one step at a time.

During my internship I worked at an emergency care shelter for emotionally disturbed adolescents. I saw tremendous pain and needs in these young people. One of the most distressing realities about their situations was that few of them had faith. I longed to talk to them about Jesus but was not permitted to because I worked for a state agency. By the time I graduated from college, I realized that I had a degree that authorized me to go into the community and help people, but I sensed in my heart I was being called to help them in a more specific way.

Helping young people and being a role model for them was very satisfying for me; however, I had a deep sense of frustration. I was unable to share the deepest part of myself, my Christian faith. They would get to know me and think (some of them anyway!) "That Cedric is a nice guy." It seemed like everything good that I did for anyone was a reflection on how good *I* was. What I want to proclaim by my life is how good **God** is! I was not sure that was getting through.

"As Jesus was setting out on his journey, a man ran up and knelt before him, and asked him, 'Good Teacher, what must I do to inherit eternal life?' Jesus replied, 'Why do you call me good? No one is good but God alone.'" (Mark 10:17-18) I always had trouble understanding that verse. Why did Jesus rebuke that man? He was only saying Jesus was good. I believe what Jesus was saying was, "Don't look at me and *my* goodness, rather see *God's goodness* flowing through me! God is the one who is good. When you see me, you see the Father."

People were seeing me, but they weren't seeing my Father. Helping people was noble and good and part of love, but for me, it had to be in the name of Christ. When I graduated from college, I made another radical decision. Through prayer and in time I decided not to look for a job in the social work field. Rather I put out feelers about doing lay ministry full time in the church. Since Vatican II, all kinds of doors have opened up for laity to become involved in ministry. I explored lay volunteer programs in the Church where I could use my social work skills and help people in the name of Jesus.

God led me to a program in the diocese of Jefferson City, Missouri. It was a program much like a Catholic Peace Corps, in which I gave a year of my life with little pay. I lived in a rectory during that year while using whatever skills I had to reach out to people. God called me to the town of about 3,000 people called Marceline, Missouri. This meant that I would leave New England for the first time in my life and move away from my parents and friends. It was scary but I stepped out in faith. I wanted to serve and love and help people.

My ministry in Marceline included teaching religion and gym class in the Catholic grade school. I also visited the elderly in their homes, as well as nursing homes and hospitals. In addition, I taught confirmation class, visited those not attending Mass and published a newsletter called "The Salt of the Earth." I was trying to be the salt of the earth as Jesus called me to be and to make people thirsty for God by my life.

WHATSOEVER YOU DO TO THE LEAST . . .

I ended up meeting the Passionists that summer when I went on a program with them to Baja California. The purpose of the program was to help the very poor of Mexico to build homes. I accompanied a group of young men who ventured down to Mexico and we spent weeks in the hot July sun reaching out to people the best we could. We mostly dug ditches and laid cement foundations for homes. That was the first time in my life I had ever seen a palm tree. That was also the first time in my life I had ever seen abject poverty. It was terrible. It was hot and dusty and the people lived in cardboard huts.

One day there were a lot of children gathered around for one of our celebrations. As I was looking at the kids all running around us, I sensed the Holy Spirit tell me, "You could have just as easily been born here. You could have been one of these children with little food, clothing and opportunity. Realize how blessed you are!" I will never forget that moment. Whenever I feel down, I remember how much I do have. That is one of the major lessons I learned in Mexico. We have so much here in the United States!

The other major lesson I learned is that I continued to be uncomfortable. True, I was digging ditches and pouring concrete in the name of Christ, but it wasn't enough. For me, I sensed that I needed to give more explicit proclamation of the Good News. People were seeing me, but were they seeing Christ?

I continued to serve as a lay volunteer for another year in 1982, in an even smaller town called Chamois, Missouri. I reached out by helping youth and elderly in various ways. In 1983 I became a salaried youth minister in St. Louis, Missouri at Chaminade High School. I started up a youth group and lived as a Prefect in the dormitory at the school. While that was meaningful (as well as tough), I knew that God was calling me to an even more explicit proclamation of the Gospel message. I sensed through time and in prayer that God was calling me to love people by becoming a priest. I was very attracted to preaching and spreading the Good News of God's love for us.

In 1983-84 I began residing with the Passionists and finally found a life-style that fulfilled my deepest desires. In the Passionist community, I found a home that would allow me to spend time with God and explicitly proclaim Jesus Christ. God was molding me and shaping me through those years in college and in Missouri and setting me apart for himself. My desires, motivations and thoughts were changing and becoming ever more refined. Now I love people not so much by digging ditches for them as digging into their hearts through the spoken word. What tremendous meaning and significance helping people brings! If you want to live passionately, you must reach out to others and serve. When you lose yourself, you actually find yourself. If you are trying to discern what God wants for you to do, step out little by little and find out! You will discover God's will one step at a time. Doors will open or remain closed as God's specific will for your life unfolds.

JUST DO IT!

It is easy to become paralyzed and do nothing when we see the tremendous needs that are in our world. There is hunger, poverty, homelessness, people not going to church, crime, violence, injustice of every form, family breakups, abortions, suicides, drug abuse, etc. Some think that because they can't do everything, they can do nothing. It is easy to become overwhelmed by the multitude of needs out there. I always tell people, pick ONE need and dedicate yourself to that. I can't do everything in my priesthood, but I can do something! I'm not going to let the fact that I can't meet every need stop me from meeting any need. Mother Teresa said, "We may not do great things but we can do small things with great love." Pray about this, and God will show you what *you* can do.

† Chapter 10 †

I heard a story about Sam Jones, an evangelist. He used to have as a part of his evangelistic campaigns what he called a "quitting service." He would issue the invitation for people to come forward and confess the sins that they were quitting. A man would come down the aisle to say, "Preacher, I'm a drinking man and I'm going to quit." A woman would come down the aisle and say, "Preacher, I've been a gossip and I'm going to quit." Another would come down the aisle to say, "I've been unfaithful to my partner and I'm going to quit." Then a lady came down the aisle to make a decision. The pastor asked her what sin she wanted to quit. She said, "Pastor, I ain't been doing nothing and I'm going to quit."

The great commission to "Go" has often become the great "omission" in our Church. Don't be overwhelmed and paralyzed. A major part of holiness and living passionately is to reach out and go. When Isaiah encountered God, he was told to go! When Peter experienced Christ at the Sea of Galilee he was told he would be a fisher of men and women. When Moses encountered God at the burning bush, God told him that he would send him. Vatican II has proclaimed that laity are to be a leaven in the world. **You** are chosen and called. "You are a chosen race, a royal priesthood, a holy nation, God's own people, that you may declare the wonderful deeds of God who called you out of darkness into his marvelous light." (1 Peter 2:9) This inspiring verse from Peter is also quoted in one of the prefaces to the Eucharistic prayer for Sunday Mass. I saw a sign outside a church building once that read, "We're a *going* church for a *coming* Lord!"

One thing that has become clearer to me is the second half of the love command, "Love your neighbor as yourself." I have heard it said that you can't love your neighbor if you don't love yourself. That may be true, but what the Lord has also taught me is that you can't love yourself if you don't love your neighbor. If you are harsh and critical and judgmental and angry, like a boomerang, these attitudes will come back to haunt you. If you don't reach out and love, you will never really love yourself. You may think you have self love if you are selfish and greedy, but deep down, you will never respect and love yourself. Loving others and serving others is the highest nobility. It was only when I began to go outside myself and reach out that I began to truly respect myself. We are made for love and if you do not love others, you cannot love yourself. If you want to be holy and set apart for God, this is a must! If you want to live passionately, reach out and touch someone! It will help you to get your worries and troubles off your mind.

11
TRIALS ARE NECESSARY
"You must realize that to reach a great union with God by way of holy love, trials are necessary."
(St. Paul of the Cross)

GRACE AND COOPERATION

Holiness is not something zapped into us, it comes through real life and God's grace. It takes time and prayer. It is a mixture of God and our sufferings, confusion, and cooperation. We must take responsibility for our part in the process and God will do the rest. I have realized over the years that it is a step by step process and God is never quite done with us. We can always give God more and more. Holiness is **both** received and achieved!

I have found that there are two main categories of believers. First, some say that in the beginning God created and then he rested. This "rest" means to them that he has taken his hands off of creation. Consider a grandfather clock. These people see God as the masterful clock maker, creating it and setting it in motion. From the moment the clock maker lets the pendulum go, he simply stands back and watches the back and forth motion, without interfering. Some see God as creating, setting the universe in motion, and then stepping back to let it play itself out.

People who believe this put a huge emphasis on their own responsibility and live by the philosophy that all depends on them. God will somehow bless their efforts. Does God really change things in response to prayer?

Probably not, some reason to themselves. Yes, God is there somehow and in some way, but if change is to occur, **we** must effect it. People like this try to force the issue, wondering if God will ever respond to their prayers for change. Because God seems slow to answer prayer, sometimes a person has to shout to be heard!

I like the story of the 14-year-old boy who was in his bedroom praying. Christmas was coming up and he was in his bedroom shouting his prayer loudly: "Lord, God, for Christmas, I want a laptop computer and a laser printer!" His twin brother came running into the room saying, "What are you shouting for? God ain't deaf!" "Yeah, but Grandma is!" came the reply.

The other category of believer says that, yes, God created the world and all that is in the universe. However, far from setting it in motion and stepping back to watch, God has a *hands on* approach. God is **at work** in creation, mysteriously and marvelously. God is involved, moving, and intricately, intimately intertwined with us. Like the story in Genesis 2:7, where God played in the mud, God is still getting his hands dirty in the muck of our lives. God is still breathing into us and recreating.

There is no doubt from the Gospels that Jesus knew God was intimately involved and touching lives. Jesus said, "My father is working still and I am working." (John 5:17) In Jesus' balanced approach, he knew God was at work, yet Jesus didn't just sit back to watch. Jesus knew that as he worked, God was actually working through him and that God was at work in creation still. Every morning we religious and priests pray the morning liturgy of the hours. Each Friday morning we pray, "*Create* in me a new heart O God . . ." (Psalm 51)

It is clear if you read the Bible that, in mysterious ways, God is actively at work in creation. God *is* involved in our life. Yes, we should take responsibility for changing our world, but ultimately it is God doing the changing. We need to have an approach that allows for both our activity and God's. We shouldn't try to do it all ourselves. On the other hand, we shouldn't just passively sit back and think that God will do everything. I like the phrase, "Work as if all depended on you, but know that all depends on God." There is a time to take responsibility and take action, and also a time to wait in trust for God to move. We need wisdom to know which is which. God absolutely answers prayer and uses us as co-creators and partners in creation.

GOD IS THE POTTER AND WE ARE THE CLAY
(Isaiah 64:8)

Isaiah 64:8 is one of my favorite verses in the Scriptures that demonstrates God's activity in creation. "O Lord, you are our Father; we are the clay and you are our potter; we are all the work of your hand." A father is one who creates. In Isaiah's view, God is a Father who **recreates**. God molds and shapes and invests himself in our lives. When I talk about God's activity in the world, I am especially talking about his sanctifying activity in our lives. It is a wonderful mixture of grace and our cooperation. I'd like to share a story that demonstrates God's recreating activity in his overall plan for our lives.

There was a married couple who used to go to England to shop in the beautiful antique stores. They both liked antiques and pottery and especially teacups. On their twenty-fifth anniversary they went to England looking for that one special teacup to celebrate their years together.

† Chapter 11 †

One day, as they were browsing, they entered an antique store and looked around. There, up on a high shelf, with spotlights on it, something caught their eye. It was the most beautiful, magnificent teacup they had ever seen. As they admired it and commented about its exquisite beauty, suddenly, they heard the teacup talk to them.

"I haven't always been like this," the teacup said. "In fact, there was a time when no one wanted me. I wasn't attractive at all. I was an old grey lump of clay. Then one day the master potter came over to me and picked me up and began to mold me and shape me and pinch me and pat me. 'Ouch', I said, 'Leave me alone.' But he only smiled and said, 'Not yet.'

"Then he took me and stretched me and put me on this wheel. Around and around and around I went. I got so dizzy. 'Let me off,' I cried. He shook his head and said, 'Not yet.' After he took me off, he put me in an oven. This is called the first firing. I never felt such heat in my life. I wondered why he was trying to burn me. I saw him looking at me through the glass in the oven door. 'Get me out of here!' I shouted. 'Not yet' was his reply.

"Finally the door opened. He took me out and put me on a shelf. I began to cool. Then nothing happened for a long time and I thought, 'When is he going to get me off this shelf?' Just then, he came over to me with all this stinky, sticky paint. Then he brushed me and painted me all over. I coughed and gagged as he painted me. I hated the smell and said, 'Stop it!' 'Not yet,' he said.

"Next he put me back in the oven. This is called the second firing. It was twice as hot as the first time and this time I knew I would suffocate. I absolutely couldn't breathe and it was so hot I thought I would melt. 'Please,' I pleaded, 'You have to get me out of here NOW!' I could see him looking at me through the glass and he shook his head and said, 'Not yet.'

"I thought that was it. I couldn't stand it anymore. I was going to die. Suddenly, the door opened and he took me out and placed me back on the shelf. Then a little while later he gave me a mirror. I looked at myself and I could hardly believe my eyes. I had completely changed. I was beautiful. Once no one wanted me, but now I am valuable and expensive and everyone admires me and wants me. Now I'm different."

I like this story because it speaks to me about my own life experiences. Scripture teaches us that God is the potter and we are the clay. One of the major truths this story about the teacup teaches is that while the teacup was going through difficulties, it didn't know that each difficulty had purpose and meaning and was for its own good.

As I look back on my ministry and general life experiences, I can see the hand of God shaping me and molding me. God uses people, circumstances and events of our lives to do this. I have felt like I was being stretched many times in my ministry. I have felt the heat of pressure. I have felt at times like I was on a shelf and nothing was happening in my life (God knows exactly what our shelf life is!) The trials and tribulations that have come my way hurt. But with the eyes of faith, I see the master potter at work, with a purpose. God knows *exactly*, *precisely* how much stretching we need; how long we need to be on the shelf and how hot to turn up the fire. God is a *master* potter.

I have learned to trust and know that God is behind all the circumstances and situations of my life. I love Psalm 31:15, "My times are in your hand." We are in God's hands.

GOD'S NOT DONE WITH ME YET!

The teacup story also teaches us that while God is interested in our everyday lives, God is also very interested in the **end product**. Our whole life is a process of growth. I saw a bumper sticker once that said, "Be patient with me, God's not done with me yet!" I love that. We are on the way. The Gospels are formulated in the structure of the journey of Jesus to Jerusalem. We are *journeying* toward wholeness and holiness. God is very patient and is willing to wait for us and stay with us. God does not give up easily. He has his eyes toward the end product–our sanctification.

When I was a sophomore in college one of the courses in my curriculum was a course in art appreciation. Since I knew so little about art, I thought I would take the course as a free elective to help round me out. I learned all kinds of things about a variety of artists from various periods. What troubled me greatly about the course was that there were no quizzes or tests along the way. There was only one criterion for our grade, the final exam.

The final exam consisted of looking at a work of art and explaining everything that we had learned in the course that might apply to it. We were to examine it and determine the possible artist, time of origin, place and other realities that went into the painting. The teacher would be able to tell by our evaluation of the art work how well we had learned our lessons. In other words, it wasn't our beginning lack of knowledge and understanding of art that we were graded on. What the teacher was interested in was our *final* understanding and appreciation of art. Luckily, I did learn as I went through the semester and did well on the one test we had at the end!

Similarly, God is at work in us now trying to make us someone magnificent. God is interested in the little tests that we have now, but is most interested in the *final product*. I once heard a quote that I love. "What we are is God's gift to us. *Who we become* is our gift to God." Of course, who we become is a mixture of our efforts *and* God's masterful hand. God is interested in our becoming. In order to live passionately, we must have the goal of becoming a beautiful, magnificent person. This is the purpose of our life. God has revealed to me that more than any ministry I do, God is interested in the type of person I am becoming through the ministry.

One other major point of the teacup story is that the teacup suffered. When we are going through things, often we don't understand what is happening. Reality doesn't seem to make sense. But the overriding principle we must live by is that God is at work in the situation. There are no drive through breakthroughs. There is no microwave maturity. Things take time, and suffering and tribulations produce a great work in us. Paul penned this beautiful verse, "We rejoice in our sufferings, knowing that suffering produces *endurance*, and endurance produces *character*." (Romans 5:3-4)

There is no other way to get endurance than by enduring things. I like to run three miles every other day. It helps me cope with stress and keeps my body in shape. I try to run fast enough to run eight minute miles. Usually about one mile into the run my body starts making its presence known. It will start to shout out to me, "This hurts, when are we going to stop?" If I stop just because I am winded or tired or hurting, I never gain the ability to endure. When I continue, then the next time I run, I am able to run the same distance without as much pain. I have gained endurance.

Endurance is a very valuable virtue and something God requires. In the story of the teacup, there were many times when the teacup felt he had reached his limit. The master potter knew exactly what he could handle and kept saying "Not yet." Little did the teacup know that the highly prized quality of endurance was being produced.

The particular brand of deodorant I use is called "high endurance" deodorant. I like it because of its quality. It lasts. God is looking for people of quality who will last, be faithful and not give up. God is looking for people who will endure. "Let us run with **perseverance** the race that is set before us, looking to Jesus the pioneer and perfecter of our faith, who for the joy that was set before him **endured** the cross . . ." (Hebrews 12:1-2)

12
WALK THE WALK
"What a great honor that God makes us walk the same way that his own divine Son walked!"
(St. Paul of the Cross)

WHO DO PEOPLE SAY THAT I AM?
(Matthew 16:13)

In the seminary, I studied a course called Christology. Christology is basically the science of studying who the historical Jesus was. We looked at the role his culture had on his life. We looked at the Jewish religion and how Jesus of Nazareth would have practiced it. More importantly for my concern here, we looked at the divinity/humanity mix of Jesus. How was he human? How was he divine? What did that mean? Some traditions of Scripture emphasize the divinity of Christ while others emphasize his humanity.

Some people think Jesus of Nazareth was born knowing everything about himself and God and the world. Since he was divine and the Word made flesh, he would be all-knowing. In other words, right from the moment of his birth, Jesus grew up knowing God's plan for him and he understood the mysteries of the universe. In theological language, this is called a "high Christology." The emphasis is on the ***divinity*** of Christ. The Gospel of John represents this train of thought. If you read carefully through the Passion narrative in John you will see that Jesus is largely in control of his destiny and doesn't even suffer at the cross. It is he who "yields" up his spirit to God. No one takes his life from him, *he* gives it to God. (John 10:18)

Others stress the humanity of Christ. Jesus, after all, was born a human being with boundaries and limited abilities. He didn't understand everything about himself and God's call on his life. Like other humans, all this unfolded before him as he walked out God's plan. Most biblical scholars, for example, tell us that the three Passion predictions (Mark 8:31, 9:31, 10:33-34) were later additions that the Gospel writers themselves provided in retrospect. Jesus himself may not have known what was going to happen to him at all. Of course, this represents the idea of Jesus as fully human and in theological terms this is called "low Christology."

Great theological debates and arguments have ensued about the important subject of the humanity/divinity of Christ. Movies and plays emphasize one or the other of the aspects of Christ's nature. Our Church teaches that in some mysterious way Jesus of Nazareth was fully human *and* fully divine. Similarly, we are graced to be fully human and fully divine. During the Eucharist, at the preparation of the gifts, the priest will pour a little water into the wine. At that moment he prays this prayer, "By the mingling of this water and wine may we who share in the humanity of Christ come to share in his divinity."

Exactly what this mysterious mix of the humanity/divinity of Christ is, no one knows for sure. We have glimpses of both by looking at our own experiences. There are times of confusion, fear and doubt. There are also moments of inspiration and leading by the Holy Spirit. Prayerful reflection on this leads to deeper knowledge of who Jesus is.

One story that raises the Christological question is from Mark 8:27-31. "And Jesus went on with his disciples to the villages of Caesarea Philippi and on the way he asked his disciples, 'Who do people say that I am?' And they told him, 'John the Baptist; and others say Elijah; and others one of the prophets.' And he asked them, 'But who do you say that I am?' Peter answered him, 'You are the Christ.' And he charged them to tell no one about him. And he began to teach them that the Son of Man must suffer . . ."

First of all, notice that even in Jesus' day, people didn't know who Jesus was. Even Peter, his closest friend, after Jesus' capture ironically stated, "I do not know this man of whom you speak." (Mark 14:71) Secondly, Peter gave the right answer when he said, "You are the Christ," (Christ, coming from a Greek word meaning the anointed one or the messiah) but for the wrong reason.

Jesus was often misunderstood in his ministry. Most Jews were expecting some sort of political or warrior messiah who would usher in the Kingdom of God by force. Few were looking for one who would ride into Jerusalem on a donkey. Peter gave the right answer about who Jesus was. He was the Christ. But Peter was told to keep quiet. Peter didn't understand what type of messiah Jesus was. Jesus was the messiah all right. But he began to teach his disciples that he must **suffer.** Peter began to get upset with such a human notion of God's chosen one. The fact that Jesus suffered speaks volumes to me about the divine/human mix of Jesus of Nazareth. Let's explore this more.

GROWING PAINS

It is explicitly clear from a number of places in the Bible that Jesus **grew**. Twice Luke makes this clear in chapter 2 of his Gospel. "The child grew and became strong, filled with wisdom; and the favor of God was upon him." (Luke 2:40) "Jesus increased in wisdom and years and in favor with God and people." (Luke 2:52)

Luke is simply stating the obvious about Jesus: he grew. Just like any other human being, Jesus observed, increased, learned and grew. He was one of us!

What I want to make clear here about the humanity of Jesus is what the writer of the book of Hebrews says, "Although he was a Son, he *learned obedience* through what he suffered." (Hebrews 5:8) Obedience is a word that comes from a Latin word meaning "to listen." For example, when a mother says to her child, "Will you listen to me!" She is saying, "Will you be obedient to me!" To listen to God is to be obedient to him with every fibre of our being. St. Benedict said, "Listen to God with the ears of your heart." When we truly hear, we become like God.

Jesus said, "You must be perfect as your heavenly Father is perfect." (Matthew 5:48) Far from burdening us with more stringent duties and laws, Jesus was saying "become like God." God is perfect in love and virtue. Be completed. Be perfected. The Vatican II document on religious life, *Perfectae Caritatis* (The Perfection of Love) states that the whole goal of religious life is that its members grow and become like God.

Again, notice, Jesus learned, he grew. He didn't understand all things from his mother's womb. My main point is that Jesus grew through his suffering. In fact, in the next verse and in Hebrews 2:10, the author of Hebrews went so far as to say that Jesus was **perfected** through suffering.

This troubles many of you, I am sure. You may be thinking, "How can this be? Wasn't Jesus perfect already?" Well, yes and no. He was perfect morally in that he never sinned. But in terms of wisdom, understanding, knowledge and virtue, he grew. If I look at my own experience, it makes perfect sense to me to know that we learn and grow and develop through suffering. This is where God gets his hands dirty in our lives. He reaches into the muck and mire of our pain and is at work *growing us up*.

SUFFERING PRODUCES CHARACTER
(Romans 5:3-4)

Sanctification is the process of making us people of character. I didn't say that God wants us to be a character, I said that God wants good character from us. As I quoted in Romans 5:3-4 above, "suffering produces . . . character."

If you read any of the lives of the saints (the word saint means "holy one") you will see that they suffered. One of my favorite saints is the founder of the Passionists, St. Paul of the Cross (Paul Daneo). Paul certainly went through many trials and tribulations in founding the Passionist community. He experienced doubts, turmoil and rejection. Yet, he persevered and endured. He matured as he went through.

One major area of suffering for Paul was in his prayer life. He lived to be 81 years old and for the majority of his life, he experienced spiritual aridity. He felt dryness and little comfort in his prayer. This would make many people give up. But he saw it as the means that God was using to make him get more deeply rooted in Christ. This also made Paul an understanding and profoundly insightful spiritual director. In addition, God was developing faithfulness, fidelity, steadfastness and long suffering in Paul. All this came through his suffering.

Who is your favorite saint? Read the story of his or her life. You will see one constant: ***suffering***. Whatever form it took, that suffering somehow purified the person and graced him or her with maturity. Suffering can work in our life to "grow us up" as well.

13
MEMORY OF THE PASSION

"Above all, I ask the good Jesus to impress upon your heart a continuous, tender and devout memory of his most sacred Passion." (St. Paul of the Cross)

WHY GOD? WHY?

I have the privilege of travelling the U.S. and Canada preaching evangelistic missions. I meet thousands of people each year. Many people come to me in the confessional and in counseling. I am constantly amazed at the amount of pain and suffering I encounter in people's lives. As a minister, I see myself wading into a sea of suffering.

It distresses me to meet good, faithful Catholics who go to Church each day or week and are suffering greatly. Suffering takes many forms. It could be the mother who just lost her son to AIDS. Possibly a man just admitted to himself that he is an alcoholic. It could be the widow who lost her husband of 52 years and now is lonely and depressed. Some find out they have cancer and have to undergo radiation therapy. Others have money problems. One common suffering I find is that parents have children who leave the faith. That devastates many hearts and ravages families. A person may come to me with doubts about the reality and validity of Christianity. Some have just gone through divorce. Still others deal with relationship problems. There is a multitude of suffering in people's lives. Everyone has something that they are dealing with.

† Chapter 13 †

The area of suffering is a topic near and dear to my heart because I am a Passionist. Remember that our "charism" or gift to the Church is that of meditating on the sufferings of Christ and proclaiming their meaning. The word passion means suffering.

We meditate on the sufferings of Christ when we reflect on his *historical* Passion 2,000 years ago. In addition, I became aware of another facet of the Passion since joining this community called the *"contemporary passion."* The contemporary passion is the suffering that Jesus is enduring in his people today. 1 Corinthians 12:27 teaches us that we are the body of Christ. Jesus is still suffering in his body. The Passion continues in us!

I realized this powerfully when I attended a slide show about the Stations of the Cross. First, an aspect of Jesus' passion was presented, say, Jesus takes up his cross. Then, split screen, a homeless person shivering in the cold was shown. Next, Jesus falls for the first time. Then, split screen, a young person was shown smoking marijuana. Later, Jesus' death on the cross was shown. Then, split screen, the atomic bomb of Hiroshima.

There are so many ways the Passion of Jesus continues in our world today: wars, poverty, homelessness, abortion, abuse, the pollution of our environment, disease, hunger, sicknesses, disasters, apathy, and injustices of every form. All these realities contribute to the suffering that Jesus still undergoes in his body the Church.

In addition, as a minister, I know that I experience suffering in many forms. The suffering that I undergo is the continuation of the Passion of Christ in me. There are the travails of travel, the hardships of life, feeling out of control, loneliness, being judged and sometimes rejected when I speak, and feeling stripped at times.

In some mystical way, Jesus is working in and through my sufferings to spread the good news of salvation and truth to the people. Paul speaks of this in Colossians 1:24, "Now I rejoice in my sufferings for your sake, and in my flesh I complete what is lacking in Christ's afflictions for the sake of his body, the church." This phrase "lacking" does not mean that Christ's sufferings in his flesh were insufficient to redeem us. Rather it means that what the historical Jesus could not do because of the limitations of time and space in his physical body, he does through his ministers everywhere down throughout the ages. I have the privilege of suffering for Jesus and when I do, mysteriously, Christ suffers in me.

THAT THEY MAY BE ONE
(John 17:22)

My point in all of this is that Jesus still suffers in you and in me. This is the contemporary passion. As a minister I know that when I suffer, I am mystically united to Jesus and I suffer for a reason. That reason is to complete what Christ was physically unable to do in the flesh — to spread the Good News in our time and place. Also, my sufferings mystically **unite me to Jesus**. Our founder St. Paul of the Cross taught that the cross was the door, as it were, to mystical union with God.

Paul had a wonderful insight. Why not look precisely at what saves us (the Cross) and **use it** as a means of communion with God. If God placed such an emphasis on a man dying on a tree to redeem us, think what it could do in our everyday prayer life and life experience. I find that when I suffer serving Jesus, my "selfish" self dies and Christ takes more and more of me. I sense a deeper oneness with Christ. As I come to him in prayer, in my poverty, I find my heart open and his presence close at hand. In some unknown way, suffering is the door to deeper union and intimacy with Christ.

Whenever I meet someone on the road and hear stories of pain and tribulation, I can't help but squirm. Sometimes I will listen to people's stories and see their flowing tears and I will struggle inside. I'll think, "He or she seems like such a good, faithful person. Why does this person have to suffer so? Why do bad things happen to good people?" In my heart of hearts I will shout, "There has to be some reason, some meaning, some purpose for the pain!" There is.

I do not want to be so arrogant as to suggest that I have the answers to the meaning of your pain. Suffering is a profound mystery. The only person who can understand the meaning of your suffering is, ultimately, *you*. As you spend time sifting through your life experience by reflecting, meditating and praying, God will help you see the meaning of what you are going through. But I can offer you some *perspectives* now that can help you to interpret the realities that you are experiencing. As I have suffered and as I have looked at the sufferings of others, I have seen some common threads that have made a lot of sense to me. I offer these threads to you as a means of helping you learn the significance of, and ways to cope with, your pain.

WHY DID GOD GIVE ME THIS?

First of all I want to declare that I do not believe that God sends suffering. Many have an image of God that is harsh and punishing. There was an emphasis on preaching in the past that stressed wrath, punishment and God as the cause of pain. Remember God is about saving the world, not condemning it! (John 3:17)

Suffering does come into *everyone's* life, however. Whether you are a faithful Christian or the worst sinner, you will suffer. Even Jesus went through trials and tribulations and deep suffering. Even the Son of God had to die. Pain, sickness and tribulation is part and parcel of being human. We were born into a chaotic, unpredictable world. Reality dictates that all of us experience sickness, all of us have trials and tribulations, and all of us will one day die. We live in a death-denying culture. We like to anesthetize pain and hide away our elderly in homes. If we get them out of sight, perhaps we won't have to deal with their suffering and face our own mortality. (Of course, there is a time when a person needs full time care.)

TO BE OR NOT TO BE?

As sobering as all this is, I'd rather be born into a world of suffering and death, than never to have been born at all! Life is precious and worth living, even if the quality of life is seemingly diminished by pain. I'm glad I have been born, even though it means that one day I will die. Better to have lived and loved than to never have lived at all.

God does not inflict us with suffering; rather, God *uses* the inevitable suffering we will encounter to bring out good.

If you reflect deeply on the Cross you will understand that God did not crucify Jesus. (Jesus saw God at work in it all however. (John 18:11)) It was a series of unjust judgments and evil motives in people that led to Jesus' being crucified. However, God brought *resurrection* out of death. That seems to be the way God always works. When there is evil present, God brings new life. As I have said before, "God writes straight with crooked lines."

Sometimes people will come up to me and say, "I don't know why God gave my son cancer." Or, "I don't understand why God took my daughter at such an early age." First of all, statements like these display faith. They show that the person making these statements believes that God is *at work* in their loved one's life. But God does not *give* cancer or sickness. Illness is the result of being human and being born into this chaotic jumble of various genes and chromosomes and family histories.

God is at work in these situations bringing about good and new life. Transformation and rebirth can occur. Other people can be affected by one person's death or pain. The effects of suffering and death are far reaching and deeper than what meets the eye. I will explore this in more detail later.

When I speak of suffering, you must understand that I mean *unavoidable* suffering. If you can avoid the pain, by all means do so. Life gives us enough trials. We don't need to be searching for them. For example, if you have a headache, please don't think, "Fr. Cedric said that suffering is good, I'm just going to wait this out and it'll make me holy." No, take an aspirin and get rid of it. God works through aspirins and doctors and other means to bring healing. Or, if you break your finger, don't put up with the pain. Go to a doctor and get it taken care of.

When I refer to "unavoidable" pain, I mean, for example, finding out that you have cancer and the ensuing treatment. Other forms of unavoidable suffering are money problems, relationship problems, deaths in the family, loneliness, despair, discovering you are homosexual, alcoholic, or addicted. It is this type of suffering that can be unavoidable in a person's life and must be dealt with. It cannot be denied. It looks you square in the face and says, "What are you going to do with me?"

You may be thinking, "Fr. Cedric, don't you believe in healing?" Yes I do, absolutely. I believe that God is our healer. I have seen people healed of all kinds of maladies at religious services I've attended. I pray for healing for people all the time and believe that God will do something in the person, but 99.999% of the time, God doesn't *cure* the person. There must be a reason for this.

Whenever I preside at an anointing of the sick service on one of my missions, I make a distinction about healing. When most hear about healing, they think *physical cure*. Many pilgrims travel thousands of miles to places like Fatima and Lourdes to experience this. Crutches are thrown aside and wheelchairs are left behind and miracles happen! I believe this.

The distinction I want to make is that there is a difference between cure and healing. A cure is physical and transient. Healing, however, is something much deeper. Healing brings wholeness and holiness and is transformative. Healing is transcendent and lasts. Healing isn't just physical but has to do with the mind, attitude, emotions and spirit. Cures fade, healings last. I believe that if it is in that person's best interest, God will cure him or her, but what God is ultimately after is healing, especially within the heart.

When people attend a healing service, I attempt to stir up their faith that God can do anything. Nothing is impossible with God. A person who was wheeled in sick can dance out cured. In addition to this, I proclaim, don't miss what God will do *within* you. God is a healing God. God desires your salvation and transformation. Simply because you haven't been "cured," don't think that nothing has happened. God has his finger on you and will not leave you.

As the sacrament is ministered to a person and he or she is anointed with the holy oil, the emphasis in the prayer is on help, mercy, salvation and "being raised up." Expect the help of God to cure you or comfort you in your affliction. You will find that you are not alone. There is a deep mercy at work in you. Have faith that your attitude, mind and emotions are being raised up. Resurrection life is coursing through your soul. Trust that your sins are forgiven and you are saved in Christ. Know that God is touching you and you will never be the same.

14
CHOOSE THE CROSS
"The cross is the way to paradise, but only when it is borne willingly."
(St. Paul of the Cross)

CHOOSE THIS DAY WHOM YOU WILL SERVE
(Joshua 24:15)

An important point that I want to make about suffering is that it forces us to make a choice. No, we don't have a choice whether or not we will suffer, but we do have a choice about *how we handle* and *react* to our suffering.

I've met people who seem to love to mope. The biblical character Job has no problems compared to theirs! They walk around depressed, down and discouraged. They have the attitude, "Woe is me, things are so hard in life. The weather is lousy. Nothing is happening." I dislike being around people like that because they drag a person down. I don't want whatever they have in them to rub off on me. However, even if you have to be around people like that, you can choose not to be like them!

I've also been around people who are suffering greatly with a buoyant spirit. You can see the smile on their face, the light in their eyes and the joy in their heart. You can't help think to yourself, "They have all this suffering in their lives, what makes this person tick?" What makes them tick is the *decision* to be the way they are. If you got up on the "wrong side of the bed" this morning, you *decided* to get up on the wrong side of the bed.

People are the way they are because of the decisions that they make. Choices become attitudes and attitudes lead to character. Remember, God wants character. Romans 5:3-4 tells us that the reason for suffering is so that we will have good character, and the fruit of a tested and tried character is a hope that will never disappoint us.

You see, the great gift that God has given us all is the gift of free will. We are not puppets on a string. We can choose. We can make decisions. We can say yes, or no. Our wills must be yielded to God. In the Our Father prayer we pray, "Your will be done." That is such a simple prayer, but it is a profound one. God has a will for our life and by grace we must choose to live in accord with this will of God.

The freedom of choice is demonstrated right from the moment a person wakes up in the morning. As you lie there, you begin to make decisions about your day. You decide when to get up. You decide what clothes to wear. You decide what goals you have for the day. You decide what you will or will not eat. You decide what you will read. You decide if and how long you will pray. You choose what to watch on TV. You choose what to talk about. You choose when you will go to bed. Many of these deliberations within are seemingly spontaneous and not thought about. But I guarantee, if you reflect on this, you will see that our life is a product of our choices. *What you do and who you become is the sum product of your decisions.*

ARE YOU BITTER OR BETTER?

Life and suffering confront us with choices. For example, say you have a child who is born mentally retarded. This can either make you bitter or better. This (or any other circumstance of suffering) can make you have a breakdown or a breakthrough! Life confronts us every day with situations that will either make us give up or give in. Suffering can be for us a prison or prism. The situations of our life and how we handle them can either be a tombstone or a stepping stone to new life. It is all up to us and our choices. How are you handling your pain and circumstances? Is your marriage making you better or bitter? Are your trials causing you to give up or give in? Do the people in your life make you feel like you are in prison, or are they a prism through which the multicolored rainbow of God's grace shines?

I have met many parents with retarded, disabled or attention deficit children. On the surface, I would think that such a situation would lead to discouragement and the desire to run away. Time and time again, however, I hear from the lips of such parents what a blessing their "special" child has turned out to be. Most look for the good and recognize God's gift. They see the patience and long suffering that is being worked in them. They wouldn't trade their child for anyone or anything. They have chosen to let their suffering make them better, not bitter.

It is the same with the marriage partner that you have chosen or, for me, religious life. I did not choose the particular people that I live in close contact with each day. I discerned a call to the vocation of religious life. I responded to a call from God. The people that I live with are a given. Some of them are easy to get along with and are very supportive. Others seem to rub me the wrong way and are difficult. I have to choose over and over again to be better and not bitter. The determining factor of your attitude is not your circumstances and sufferings, but YOU and your *reactions* to circumstances!

† Chapter 14 †

WHAT'S THE MEANING OF THIS?

A book that has had a major impact on me is *Man's Search for Meaning* by Viktor E. Frankl. In this moving account of his life in a Nazi concentration camp, Frankl graphically talks about the horrendous sufferings of starvation, nakedness, cold, humiliation and the constant threat of death. All the familiar goals of life as we know it were snatched away. What alone remained is what he calls the "last of human freedoms"–the ability to "*choose one's attitude* in a given set of circumstances."

Frankl made the stunning but true statement, "Even though conditions such as lack of sleep, insufficient food and various mental stresses may suggest that the inmates were bound to react in certain ways, in the final analysis it becomes clear that the sort of person the prisoner became was the result of an inner decision and not the result of camp influences alone." Some people looked at the suffering and threw themselves into the electric wire and gave up. Others thought of their wives and families and found purpose and meaning, and gave in to the situation with a good attitude. There is purpose and there is meaning in every situation and circumstance of our life if we choose to see it. Often others will not and cannot recognize it, but life is charged with meaning.

Because of his experiences and observations in the concentration camps, Viktor Frankl developed a theory of psychology called "logotherapy." According to logotherapy, the striving to find a ***meaning*** in one's life is the primary motivational force in man. A person is able to live and even to die for the sake of his ideals and values. If you can find meaning in your suffering, then somehow the suffering becomes less painful. Life is charged with meaning and purpose. Each person must discover this particular meaning for himself or herself.

NO GREATER LOVE
(John 15:13)

One story that illustrates perfectly what Viktor Frankl taught is the story of St. Maximilian Kolbe. Maximilian Kolbe was a Franciscan priest who lived from 1894-1941. In 1941 he was arrested by the Nazi's in Poland and sent to the concentration camp at Auschwitz. During his captivity, a fellow prisoner escaped and the commandant announced that ten men would have to die by starvation because of this. Playing judge, the commandant picked the ten men by his whim. One of the men chosen to die, Francis Gajowniczek, was a husband and father.

As the men were being marched away to the starvation bunkers, someone did something that was against the law. He stepped out of line and made a request. That someone was prisoner #16670, Fr. Maximilian Kolbe. The request he made was that he die in Gajowniczek's place. Eyewitnesses have said that when Maximilian stepped forward with such a noble request, the commandant was confused and dumbfounded. He wasn't sure what to make of this skinny priest with such boldness. Kolbe could have been killed on the spot. However in the strangeness of the startled moment, the switch was accepted and Kolbe went to die in the starvation bunker.

The ten were ordered to strip naked and the slow starvation process began. Fr. Maximilian led the prisoners in song and prayer. Then on the eve of the Assumption of Mary (Maximilian was especially devoted to Mary) the jailer came to a praying Maximilian and murdered him with carbolic acid. From the beginning, Kolbe's noble attitude was fueled by his love for Jesus and a sense of mission. He wanted to be a witness for the love of God. The camp didn't determine his attitude, rather, his attitude won many for Christ. Now, Francis Gajowniczek's mission is to travel, telling everyone about this mystic martyr who died in his place.

If you can see your life as charged with meaning, then your attitude will shift accordingly. I travel around the country as a priest preaching and helping people discover God. There is tremendous significance in what I do. Because of this, when I run into trials and difficulties and hardships, I am able to bear them more easily because I know that there is a **purpose** behind my sufferings. You don't have to be a priest to find meaning in your life. **Every** vocation is purposeful. If you are a mother with small children, taking care of them is full of meaning. If you are a father and you go to work each day for your family, that is very significant. A young person in school studying has a life charged with purpose.

DO ALL TO THE GLORY OF GOD
(1 Corinthians 10:31)

In any vocation it is easy to feel unappreciated by the people you are trying to bless and support. Sometimes I feel that way in my own community. I can be out on the road for weeks working hard and ministering and then when I return, some in the community will barely ask a question about how it went. A mother may work hard all day with the kids and then scramble to prepare a meal and her husband won't even notice how much she has done. Or a husband may return from work to stories of how hectic life around the house was. He can feel angry and unappreciated. We all go through times and seasons of feeling unappreciated by the people we are trying to love and support the most.

One verse has helped me so much. "Whatever your task, work heartily, *as serving the Lord and not people*, knowing that from the Lord you will receive the inheritance as your reward; you are serving the Lord Christ." (Colossians 3:23-24) What this verse taught me is that I must think of all the service and good that I do as to God. I cannot look for support and pats on the back from people all the time. People simply will not give them! Rather, when I serve people, I do it *as to the Lord.* (Ephesians 6:7) That has helped purify me of my need to always be thanked. Instead of getting angry and resentful when I am not thanked, I consider what I do as service done to God. I don't always need praise!

The bottom line is that God is very close to every one of us. *God* is the one who called us to the vocation we have received whether religious life, marriage, or the single life. Every vocation is very important to God and God notices every little thing that you do. Psalm 56:8 says that God has stored all our tears in a bottle. God is aware of our sufferings and service. All is written in his book. (Revelation 20:12) Jesus taught that your Father sees you "in secret" and will reward your good deeds. (Matthew 6:6)

Your life does matter! It has infinite value and worth to God. You may *feel* insignificant and not worth much. Perhaps you *feel* unappreciated and devalued; however, you have tremendous value and worth to God. Every act, every service, every deed that you do is noticed and appreciated by God. If you are struggling with being unappreciated, reorient your focus and "*do it as to the Lord.*" This gives me purpose in what I do, even when I feel no one understands me or appreciates me. In turn, I am able to have an attitude of thanks and I continue to press on because I know God notices and is for me. There is tremendous meaning in our vocations as we serve God.

I seek to glorify God by writing this book. I know that not everyone will buy and read it. Some will judge me harshly because of what is written in it. Others will disagree with my theology. Some of my own community who read it will never say a word to me about it. When I examine my own motive for writing this (and I have searched long and hard) it is to help people. I want people to come to a living relationship with Jesus and to know salvation. I want all to grow in the Lord and understand the sanctification process. I desire that everyone become a person of Godly character and integrity and gain victory in his or her life. But I write it mostly "*as to the Lord.*" I began this project because I sensed an anointing from God to do it. I wrote this book primarily to glorify God and to help people, not to get praise.

I think this idea is the notion behind this teaching from Jesus, "So you also, when you have done all that is commanded you, say, 'We are unworthy servants; we have only done what was our duty.'" (Luke 17:7-10) I always found these words of Jesus to be a bit harsh here. We are not robots without feelings. However, Jesus was talking about attitudes and motives. Serve God first. Don't necessarily look for praise. God is aware of what you are doing and it has great significance. **God** will reward you.

Serving God is the meaning and purpose that is the foundation of my whole life. If you have faith, you will see that God is close at hand and intricately involved with you. (Psalm 139) Our whole lives must be for the glory of God. Praise and thanks from others may come and that helps, but God will strip you of the extreme need of having to have human praise. When push comes to shove, our significance and the meaning in all that we do comes from serving God. That can help our attitude immensely. When you know that every deed in every waking moment is for the Lord, that colors everything. Are you self serving? Are you looking for the praise of others? Or are you serving the living God in all that you do? This Bible verse is central in my life, "So, whether you eat or drink, or *whatever* you do, *do all to the Glory of God.*" (1 Corinthians 10:31)

15
REMAIN ON THE CROSS
"How good it is to remain on the cross with Jesus."
(St. Paul of the Cross)

WHY DO BAD THINGS HAPPEN TO GOOD PEOPLE?

When it comes to attitude and how you see life, you can either be a victim or a victor. That is a choice you make. The series of continual, habitual choices you make determines your attitude. My dad teaches me a lot about attitude by the way he lives his life. As I write this, dad is 76 years old and lives with mom in Florida. I have two older sisters and I am the third child and the only boy. Originally we grew up in Agawam, Massachusetts, but my parents moved south after my sisters got married and I left the house to join the Passionists.

In the early 1940's Dad joined the United States Navy and served our country in the South Pacific during World War II. He was a coxswain in the Seabees. At one point in his military service, he was on board a communications vessel in the South Pacific. It was 1943 and he was a healthy young 19-year-old. As he was walking on the deck of the ship some maintenance workers were working on some equipment. As Dad was walking by, a hot piece of the equipment "just happened" to fly out and hit dad precisely in his left eye. It seared the pupil of his left eye shut.

Why things like that "suddenly" happen, we don't know. Accidents do happen to everyone, however, and bad things happen to good people. Dad has not had vision in his left eye for over 57 years now, all because of a split second accident. The finest laser surgeons have tried to open the eye and restore vision in it, all to no avail. My dad has lost vision in that eye and is a disabled veteran.

Imagine for a moment going through life with one eye. Try driving a car with one eye closed (on second thought, don't!) You lose your peripheral vision. The three-dimensionality of life fades. You are half blind. Life is much more difficult. It is hard to drive, work and see things.

My dad has always been an inspiration in my life. First of all, he is one of the most generous and patient people I have ever met. I believe that some of this attitude of his was forged through his suffering. Also, he never took his misfortune out on me, my mother or my sisters. I never heard him complain about it. I never sensed any misplaced anger on us because of it. Rather, the suffering he bore tempered him and refined him into a gentle person. My father is a gentleman.

I am not saying bite the bullet and suffer bravely whatever comes your way; rather, suffering, as it comes to everyone, will temper your temper and transform you into a person of character. We are forged on the anvil of life's experiences. You can either have a victim mentality about life or a victor's mentality about your experience. Sooner or later one must take responsibility for one's own life and go forward.

My father also inspired me another way. When he was honorably discharged from the military he became a carpenter. Most people can't do carpentry well with two eyes and dad did it with one. He has a wonderful skill to work well with wood and to work with his hands. He used to build houses and additions to houses as well as cabinets and other fine interior work. I've seen him do lecterns and altars and other woodworking for churches. He was a master craftsman. I know because I used to work with him as a teenager.

Oh, by the way, that's how I knew I had a call to the priesthood: I was a lousy carpenter, let me tell you! I wonder if that's what happened to Jesus? My father has an exquisite ability to work with his hands, and I don't. I would always struggle with carpentry and get frustrated. My bodily abilities lie more in movement and athletics rather than things mechanical.

What my father showed me is that hard circumstances and negative happenings don't necessarily determine what you become. The choice is up to you. You can either be a victim or a victor in life. Your *irritations* can be *invitations* to new life. There are scores of stories of people who have disabilities who have turned those "challenges" into new abilities. You can turn your tragedies into triumph. Are you grumpy or grateful? If life hands you a lemon, then make lemonade! A good attitude leads to a high altitude.

POP QUIZ

Suffering is the great teacher. We can learn a lot from our pain. One day I was driving down the street (I call it the "highway of life") and as I looked down on the pavement I saw the word "SCHOOL" painted in big white letters. Children who are picked up on school buses each day aren't the only ones going to school. I don't know what level of education you may have attained. You may have graduated from grammar school, high school, college, graduate school or more. Whatever your education level is, you didn't stop going to school the day you graduated. We are *all* going to school, *every day*.

I once saw a bumper sticker that read, "The truly educated person *never* stops going to school." I like that, because life is about learning and growing *all the time*. One of the purposes of each day is to learn. The truth about God's school, however, is that we *keep* taking tests. There is really no flunking out. If we don't pass it the first time we just keep taking it over and over again.

IS THERE STILL A PURGATORY?

Speaking of never flunking out, I'd like to say a word about purgatory. We are learning and being purified on earth. The motivation for sanctification is not to *merit* salvation. As I have already discussed, we are saved by faith by what Jesus did for us on the Cross. Our motivation ought to be becoming Christ-like, glorifying God and doing what pleases God. We become holy not to earn heaven, but to draw closer to God and become like God. 1 John 3:3 states, "Everyone who has the hope (of seeing God) purifies themselves as God is pure."

One of the major reasons we are being sanctified, purified and purged of our sinfulness is so that we will be **able to receive God** ever more fully. We are able to receive God to a certain extent now through a faith pregnant with works. After we die, the more pure we have become, the more *intensely* we will be able to receive the glory, ecstacy and love of God. Sin, unholiness and character flaws are a hindrance to receiving the tremendous joy and rapture of the beatific vision.

That is why purgatory is a grace. We have a tradition of praying for the "poor" souls in purgatory. Well, actually they are rich! They are saved, but somehow, someway, through the favor of God they are being further purified so that they will be able to receive even more of God and experience more intensely the delights of Heaven. Our capacity to receive love and experience it is elastic. Our hearts are expandable. Sanctification renders us open to receive. In Matthew 11:11, Jesus talks about people who are "least" in the kingdom of heaven. This implies that there are different degrees or states even in heaven. I believe what he meant is that various people will have different capacities to enjoy and receive God. Those who are purified and love on earth will be able to receive love and joy in a more intense way. Give and it will be given to you! These are the "greater" in the kingdom.

The Catechism of the Catholic Church #1030 talks about purgatory as a grace. "All who die in God's grace and friendship, but still imperfectly purified, are indeed assured of their eternal salvation; but after death they undergo purification, so as to achieve the holiness necessary to enter the joy of heaven." Notice, these people are saved. They are going to heaven because of what Jesus did for them; however, God gives them an opportunity to "learn" and grow more so that they will enter more joy in heaven.

For years I struggled with this doctrine of our Catholic Church. As I reflect on my own experience and grow and learn, purgatory makes a lot of sense. Our Church has two thousand years of wisdom and tradition. I revere that. Don't think of purgatory as a place where people are screaming out in flames; rather, think of a reality where the "fire" of the Holy Spirit continues to purify. (Luke 3:16) Far from being poor, these saved souls are given *more time to lea*rn, grow and receive God ever more fully. Sometimes we just need more time. I don't know about you, but I want to learn my lessons well now, on earth. I'm not the type that likes to "stay after school."

VIRTUE HAS ITS REWARDS

Just what are we supposed to learn? *Virtue*. Some think virtue went out the window at Vatican II. The reason why the windows of Vatican II were "opened" was not to let virtue out, but to let *in* the breath of fresh air that is the Holy Spirit! Virtue is still valid and very much alive in Catholic teaching. I invite you to read *The Catechism of the Catholic Church* #1803. "A virtue is an habitual and firm disposition to do the good. It allows the person not only to perform good acts, but to give the best of himself. The virtuous person tends toward the good with all his sensory and spiritual powers; he (or she) pursues the good and chooses it in concrete actions." St. Gregory of Nyssa is quoted in the catechism, "The goal of a virtuous life is to become like God."

Notice that virtues are habitual. They are patterns of goodness that we repeat, good habits if you will. Also, the will is involved. We choose to do good in concrete actions. Lastly, if you read on in the Catechism, you will see that virtue has to do with attitudes. They are "*firm attitudes, stable dispositions* . . . that govern our actions." (#1804) This is what God is after. God is extremely interested in an attitude that is good and consistent. God desires stable and mature emotions and moods. The Holy Spirit comes to purify our thought life and our wills. God desires the character of Jesus Christ in us.

Virtue is praised in many places in the Bible. The Book of Wisdom says, "In the memory of virtue is *immortality* . . . and throughout all time it marches crowned in triumph, victor in the contest." (Wisdom 4:1-2) Virtue exalts those who practice it, but those without virtue will be lost. "As when an arrow is shot at a target, the air, thus divided, comes together at once, so that no one knows where it went. So we (the unvirtuous) also, as soon as we were born, ceased to be, and we had no sign of virtue to show, but were consumed in our wickedness." (Wisdom 5:12-13) Scripture makes it clear that virtue is true treasure and has infinite value.

Some examples of virtue are: love, hope, courage, faith, patience, generosity, compassion, justice, honesty, prudence, trust, temperance, fidelity, and mercy. What is interesting is that suffering is actually the classroom that can teach us and help us to learn and develop these virtues.

THANK YOU FOR YOUR PATIENCE!

In the confessional one problem I hear confessed a lot is impatience. Patience is such a major virtue. Jesus exalted it by saying, "By patient endurance you shall gain your lives." (Luke 21:19) Jesus was never in a hurry. He was not bent out of shape. Meditate on the patience of Jesus of Nazareth as he is ridiculed and taunted on the Cross. He remained silent. He saved our lives by his patient endurance!

Patience is not waiting: everyone has to wait. Not everyone has patience; rather, patience is a matter of *how you wait*. For example, when you are at the grocery store and want to check out and there is a long line, how do you react? When you are driving and there is someone slow in front of you who makes you miss the green light, how do you react? Sometimes in airports a flight will be delayed or even canceled. It is interesting to see the reactions that people have. Some will start complaining out loud or swear or even yell at the person checking them in. (Their actions and reactions show their character development!) Some time ago my flight was delayed for eight hours because of ice storms in Dallas. The flight attendant said, "Thank you for your patience!"

We have a whole season in our Church liturgical year dedicated to waiting. It is called Advent. Interestingly, the season calls us to wait *with* joy, expectation, hope, prayer, faith and patience. Patience definitely is exercised in the everyday situations of life.

In addition, it is a major virtue to "wait well" for our dreams and goals in life to take shape. If you sense God has put some dream in your heart, there is always a season of waiting that will occur. During this season of waiting for the fulfillment of God's dream for you, your patience will be tested. You must wait with joy, expectancy, prayer, faith and hope. This is patience. You must wait well in order to inherit all that God has for you. If you get impatient and grow discouraged and doubt and sin and give up, you won't inherit anything. The writer of the letter to the Hebrews warns us about "sluggishness" and makes this poignant statement, "Be imitators of those who through faith *and patience* inherit the promises." (Hebrews 6:12)

It is your attitude while you wait that God is interested in. Life is full of situations of waiting. One verse of Scripture that has always helped me is Sirach 2:4-5, "Accept whatever is brought upon you, and in changes that humble you be patient. For gold is tested in the fire and acceptable people in the furnace of humiliation." One of the ways we learn patience is by trusting God to work out the situation. Perhaps you hear that someone has gossiped about you. Your reputation has been questioned or hurt. Don't retaliate. Don't spread further gossip about that person. Your patience is being tested. (1 Peter 2:20-25) Humiliation is the great tester of patience. Perhaps you have a "dream" from God and you've shared this dream with your spouse or friend and they laughed at you. Don't grow impatient. They weren't the one to whom God gave the dream. You are being tested. Remain patient and steadfast. Trials bring to the surface patience (or impatience, for that matter).

I heard the story of a woman, a mother of three, who went to a priest for confession. Her children were driving her crazy. They were bouncing off the walls and she was very frustrated. Finally, she had had it and went to confession to a wise old priest. "Father," she said, "I am at the end of my rope! My children are frustrating me and won't listen to me. I've had it. I am so impatient right now. Will you please pray for patience?" "Sure," the priest replied. Then he began to pray in this way: "Lord, send this woman tribulation in the morning, tribulation in the afternoon, tribulation in . . ." "Wait!" the woman interrupted. "I asked you to pray for patience, what are you doing?" "Ma'am," said the priest, "Tribulation produces patience!" (Romans 5:3)

I always say, be careful what you pray for, you might just get it! Perhaps some of you have been praying and wondering why God isn't answering your prayers. Could it be that God *is* answering your prayers, but in ways you don't understand? When you pray, look, notice and be aware. God is there. God has wisdom and knows what is best.

Weightlifters have a saying as they lift those heavy weights: "No pain, no gain." Without the pain involved in lifting the weights, the muscles will not grow big. Similarly, in our spiritual life, without the pain involved in daily struggles, our spiritual "muscles" simply will not grow.

The Catechism distinguishes between two types of virtue. One type is the "theological virtue." Faith, hope and love are examples of this type. They are "infused" into the souls of the faithful. (#1813) The other type is what the Catechism calls the human or moral virtues. The bold statement is then made, "The moral virtues are *acquired* by human *effort*." (#1804) St. Thomas Aquinas, a great doctor of the Church, said, "You get virtue by *doing* virtue." There are no shortcuts to living a virtuous life: it is work and there is nothing easy about it. That's why virtue is so valuable.

Virtue is **developed** over time. It is a process of making good choices over and over. A person can't be patient in a situation once and then be perfectly patient. It takes a *pattern* of right behaviors.

We have a fiesta at our retreat center once a year in June. I ran a vocation booth trying to interest young people in the Passionists. I came up with the idea of an "interactive" booth. My team and I hung a Passionist habit up in front of the booth with stairs behind it. Above the habit we hung a sign "Future Passionist." Then we invited any young person who wanted to, to step up on the stairs behind the habit and get his or her picture taken. When the picture was taken from the front, the habit would be seen with the young person's head above it, with the words "Future Passionist" above them.

We took the picture with an instamatic Polaroid camera. That way we could give the young person the picture right away. At first when the picture was taken you could barely see the figure, just clouded black and white. Then, soon, right before your eyes, you could see it develop. Suddenly the figure became clearer and sharper and then, soon, the picture was fully developed and given away.

Virtue *develops* in much the same way. At first it is fuzzy and unclear. You aren't sure what is in you. But in time, after habitual repeated actions and firm decisions, a particular virtue develops and becomes more focused. The image that becomes clearer and clearer is the image of Jesus Christ with your face on it.

16
SHARED SUFFERING
"We share in the joys and sorrows of our contemporaries as we journey to the Father."
(Passionist Constitutions #3)

NO MAN IS AN ISLAND

Another major virtue I would like to look at is compassion. The word compassion means to "suffer with" (passion = suffer, com = with). As a Passionist, I am extremely interested in this. If you want to live passionately, you must have compassion.

The Gospel of Luke highlights this as a major virtue. In the Sermon on the Mount in Matthew, Jesus' climax is, "Be perfect as your heavenly Father is perfect." (Matthew 5:48) Luke changes this in his sermon on the plain. In Luke 6:36 we hear Jesus emphasize, "Be merciful (compassionate for the ills of others) as your Father is merciful." Remember the story of the prodigal son in Luke 15? When the father saw the son in verse 20, he had compassion. The Greek word here means that he was "moved in the depths of his bowels." Apparently the father had suffered in his own life and he was able to identify with his son's plight. What motivated the good Samaritan in Luke 10:33 was "compassion." It was because he was moved within, apparently because he had suffered himself, that this foreigner at odds with the Jews took the risk of reaching out.

Compassion doesn't come cheaply. It is learned through suffering. When a person is young, often they don't have much compassion, simply because they haven't suffered much themselves.

Chapter 16

TURN YOUR SCARS INTO STARS

That's the way it was for me in my life. I grew up in a white middle class neighborhood in Agawam, MA. I was pretty much sheltered from suffering growing up, but one thing was an "eye opener" for me. When I was in the seventh grade I developed acne and had it all through high school. I remember how hard it was for me to go to school with red blotches on my face. It hurt my self esteem and the way I saw myself. After all, I had to "face" the world with acne. Of course the acne faded and there are some scars that still hurt, but I've learned to turn my scars into stars. The blemishes of life can be blessings!

I used to laugh at others who had acne or were different than I. But my own experience of sickness brought me humility. I began to get quiet and listen to life. It slowed me down at an early age. (This is often what suffering, in any form it may take, will do: slow a person down.) I became much more reflective. Instead of living a superficial life, I began to look deeper. Beauty is not just skin deep. There is a lot more to life than just the surface! Did God give me acne? I don't think so, but God used it to teach me and give me depth as a person.

I've learned that one of the secrets of life is to refuse to deny reality. I have a saying, *"Face it, embrace it, and God will grace it."* Paul had to learn this, too. He had a "thorn" in the flesh he had to deal with. Scholars are not quite sure what this thorn was. He asked God a number of times to remove it. God's answer to Paul and to us was, "My grace is sufficient for you, for my power is made perfect in weakness." (2 Corinthians 12:7-9) Paul learned that when he faced his pain, and embraced it, then God graced it. He became content with weakness and found that when he was weak, he was strong. (2 Corinthians 12:10) His flaws led to favor. Part of Paul's strength was his compassion. It comes as no surprise that when Paul justified himself to the Corinthian community, he listed his *sufferings* as his *credentials*. (2 Corinthians 11:23-33)

As I embraced my own pain, I began to look at other people who were suffering. I saw fat people, unpopular people, uncoordinated people, disabled people, poor people, bald people, people with diseases, people who couldn't speak well, among others. Instead of brushing them aside or not even noticing them, I could sympathize in some way. I didn't have the same suffering they may have had, but any suffering causes one to be able to somehow share with the suffering of another. Now I am interested in others, not just in myself. Believe it or not, it was a case of acne as a teenager that led me to a major awakening of compassion in my life! Suffering has helped lead me into ministry and has helped me to become an effective minister.

Reflect on your life. What has taught you? Isn't it your suffering? Don't *waste* your suffering. It is too valuable. You can see more through a tear drop than you can through a telescope! You can *be sore* or *soar*. It's up to you. John Donne wrote, "No man is an island. Every man is a piece of the continent, a part of the main." Instead of "me," it's "we." We're all in it together. Suffering will teach you, if you reflect on it. One of its major lessons is that of compassion.

It's easy to laugh at the suffering of others and not feel their pain. I like the story of the twelve year boy who was standing there holding his thumb and crying his head off. A woman came up to him and said, "Young man, why are you crying?" "Because my father hit his thumb with a hammer!" he replied. "Wait a minute," said the woman. "If your *father* hit *his* thumb with a hammer, then why are *you* crying?" "At first I wasn't crying," the boy sheepishly said. "At first I was laughing!"

There is a woman I know in California who is the mother of three children and in her late forties. She developed breast cancer that was life threatening. Because of this terrible affliction she had to undergo surgery, chemotherapy and radiation treatments. It was an awful mix of hospitals and needles and trials. She lost all her hair. She felt very sick. There was a lot of confusion and uncertainty.

Thanks be to God the woman is in remission and has recovered from cancer. The mix of prayer and the doctor's help has brought her to health. During her treatment this woman's gospel became "appreciate the now." She would tell just about everyone she saw to: "Savor your family, enjoy each moment, and notice what you have. Make each day count. Live life to the full and live passionately!" Her suffering taught her how transitory life is. Her pain taught her to treasure the people in her life even more. Cancer taught her to live more fully! Now she is a witness in her local church and in her community and inspires others to choose to live each day abundantly.

The other truth this woman has learned and preaches is that we are not in control. We may be able to control a few things in life, but for the most part, none of us are really in control of life. For example, think about this: Who of us chooses when and where we are born? Who chooses the parents they will be born to? We have no control over what kind of body we get. We don't pick whether we will be male or female. We don't determine how tall or short we will be. Who can determine what color hair we will be born with (and how long we will be able to keep it!) No one chooses what type of face he or she will have (although with plastic surgery, all this is changing). No one knows when he or she will die. These traits are pretty much givens in life. I've found that we have to *"give in"* to the *"givens"* in life.

I believe that these given "unknowns" are built in mechanisms that call us to trust. It should be obvious to us that we are not in control. Instead of learning from this, many try to grab even more tightly for control!

As I get older, I am learning that the body only lasts so long. Things wear out. A few years ago I noticed that when I was preaching, I couldn't really see the faces of the people. I knew I had to get glasses and wear them. It was hard for me, because all my life I was able to see without glasses. It took a lot of humility for me to use them publicly the first time.

Now I've noticed that my hair is beginning to turn grey in spots. Also, it seems to be thinning some. When I run, my knees hurt me at times. When I play golf my back hurts at times. Wrinkles are developing all over my body. I'm still relatively young: what's going on? I've discovered that the aging process itself is a God given, *built in process of purification* and surrender. Paul the apostle said, "We do not lose heart. Though our outer nature is wasting away, our inner nature is being renewed every day. For this slight momentary affliction is preparing for us an eternal weight of glory beyond all comparison . . ." (2 Corinthians 4:16-17)

Did you know that the highest incidence of AIDS is in older people? That's right. Senior people need hearing aids, walking aids and nursing aids!

You know you are getting older when:

- Your back goes out more than you do.
- Your knees buckle, but your belt won't.
- You get winded playing chess.
- You sit in the rocking chair and can't make it go.
- You turn out the light for economic reasons rather than romantic ones.
- Dialing long distance wears you out.

Some great things about getting older:

- Your eyes won't get much worse.
- Finally you can eat dinner at 4:00.
- Things you buy now won't wear out.
- There's nothing left to learn the hard way.
- People no longer view you as a hypochondriac.
- In a hostage situation you are likely to be released first.
- Your supply of brain cells is finally down to a manageable size.
- Your joints are more accurate than the Weather Channel.
- Your investment in health insurance is finally beginning to pay off.
- Your secrets are safe with your friends because they can't remember them either.

Surely the common experience of our bodies can make us compassionate!

ONE STEP AT A TIME

I have ministered in Twelve Step programs at various times in my career. People who participate are addicted to various behaviors, people or emotions such as overuse of alcohol, sex, food, shopping, and drugs. When you are addicted, you are "given over" or surrendered to a behavior, person or emotion. To experience recovery, one must lose control and surrender to God. People in this program, for the most part, love to be in control and experience a loss of control to their addiction. Most people who have admitted that they are addicted and that they need help have gone through some major suffering to get to that point. They have to *admit* to themselves that they need help from God and from others.

The genius of the twelve step program is that hurting people help other hurting people. Those who have been there and gone through various difficulties are the very ones who now reach out to those who are just joining the program. In twelve step meetings, those attending for the first time will hear stories that they can relate to from people who have been there. Those who have been sober for a number of years become sponsors of others. They can sympathize and have compassion. They have suffered the very same thing. Rather than waste their suffering, people in recovery *use* it to help others. That is one of the reasons why this program works!

If you want to live passionately, learn. Allow every aspect of your suffering to teach you. Examine your experience. Life is the great teacher. Learn your lessons well and perhaps you won't have to take them again!

17
LOVE IS A FIRE
"Love is a fire reaching through to the inmost soul."
(St. Paul of the Cross)

A SWORD SHALL PIERCE THROUGH YOUR SOUL (LUKE 2:35)

The virgin Mary is a wonderful example of a person who allowed life to teach her. She was taught by many things, but one of her greatest teachers was suffering. The feast day of September 15 is a very intriguing one: it is called "Our Lady of Sorrows." It is an important feast day for Passionists because Mary is the principal patroness of our congregation. We meditate on her sufferings and what we can learn from Mary.

Vatican II in its *Dogmatic Constitution on the Church* #65 calls Mary the model of virtues. "She cooperated by her obedience, faith, hope and burning charity in the work of the Savior in restoring supernatural life to souls. For this reason she is a mother to us in the order of grace." (#61)

We look at models on TV because they are beautiful. I used to make model airplanes when I was a young boy. When I was finished I would put them up on my bureau to enjoy and look at. Our Church teaches us that Mary is a *model* of virtue to look at and imitate. She is not someone to be worshiped. Whenever we hear of her appearing at Fatima, Lourdes, Medjugorje or other places, she never points to herself; rather, she is always pointing to and leading people to Jesus her Son. The Church reveres her because of her role in the plan of salvation and because she is the model of virtue. She was given to us by Jesus on the cross as our mother. (John 19:26-27) We are invited to look at her and imitate her goodness.

On my pilgrimage in 1999, our final destination was Rome. On one of the days in Rome we all walked through St. Peter's Basilica. On the right side as you enter is the famous *Pietà* by Michelangelo. This stunning statue captures the moment when, after his death, Jesus was lowered from the cross. Mary is frozen in time holding the dead body of her son, Jesus.

Can anyone imagine the pain and torment that flooded the soul of this woman? Sometimes I will meet mothers in various churches who have lost a child to suicide, AIDS, accident or sudden crib death. Their pain and loss is incredible. Mary understands, she went through it.

I saw the scene captured by the *Pietà* in the movie *Jesus of Nazareth* by Franco Zeffirelli. The movie is a wonderful portrayal of the life of Christ. Zeffirelli masterfully mixed the humanity and divinity of Christ in a way that was quite real. In the movie, as Jesus died on the cross, thunderstorms approached and it began to pour rain. When Jesus was lowered from the cross Mary received the dead body of her beloved Son. She sat there on the ground with Jesus cradled on her lap. She sobbed and looked up to heaven and wailed with sorrow. She was sopping wet because of the downpour. That moment in the movie captured for me the prophecy of Simeon, "A sword will pierce through your soul." (Luke 2:35)

We have to remember that Mary was human and had the same feelings we do. Can you imagine the doubt and confusion that filled her mind? As she held Jesus she must have wondered where God was. What about the plan of God to save people through Jesus? Everything seemed so tragic and unjust. Promises made seemed to have been broken. Yet, she believed! She trusted. She patiently endured this.

GOD WORKS FOR GOOD
(Romans 8:28)

One truth that has constantly touched my life and is foundational in my belief system is this verse from Paul's letter to the Romans. "We know that in *everything* God works *for good* with those who love him, who are called according to his purpose." (Romans 8:28) I have seen this verse done in calligraphy, framed, and hung on walls. Chapters in books have been devoted to this. Beautiful songs have been sung about Romans 8:28, and rightly so! That one verse speaks volumes.

I believe you are a person who loves God or you wouldn't be reading this book. You have been called according to his purpose. In fact, Scripture teaches that "*before the world began*, God chose us in Christ to be holy and blameless before God. God destined us in love to be his sons and daughters through Jesus Christ, according to the *purpose of his will* . . ." (Ephesians 1:4-5) Therefore, because we are called and love God, we can believe that whatever happens to us, good or bad, God will ultimately make good come out of it. This truth has comforted me and given me hope when I am confused and don't understand what is going on at a particular moment in my life. No matter what you are going through now, God has a plan and purpose and is at work!

Mary may not have understood on Good Friday what *good* could possibly come from the death of Jesus, but on Pentecost, she got a revelation. Acts 1:14 tells us that Mary was with the others when the Holy Spirit filled them on

Pentecost. A new glimpse was given into the plan of God. Jesus' tragic death and her mournful loss was to create a new humanity. God brought "good" out of "bad."

Our culture and upbringing gives us ways of looking at and interpreting the events of our lives. Basically, we have been taught that if a happening is painful, it is "bad," and if an event brings pleasure, it is "good." I think as Christians, we need wisdom to *look beyond the surface* of things to see the true meaning of reality.

FEELING LUCKY?

I heard a story that illustrates what I mean. A wise seasoned farmer had a horse that he used to till his fields. Because he was rather poor, it was his only horse. One day the harness connecting the horse to the plow broke and the horse escaped and ran away. The man's neighbors heard about this and came to him with sympathy. They said to him, "We heard about your horse running away. That's bad luck!" The farmer replied, "Bad luck? Good luck? Who knows?"

Two days later the horse returned leading a team of wild horses behind it. The people heard about it and came to him congratulating him. "Why, that's good luck!" the people said. "Good luck? Bad luck? Who knows?" was the farmer's reply.

Later, the farmer's son was attempting to tame one of the wild horses. While he was trying to "break" the horse, he was bucked off and broke his leg. Once again the neighbors heard of this and came to the farmer and said, "Too bad about your son, that's bad luck!" The farmer said, "Bad luck? Good luck? Who knows?"

The next day the army marched into town and conscripted all the able bodied young men of the town to go to war and fight. Because the son had a broken leg, they left him alone. Now, was that good luck or bad luck?

We need wisdom and insight to look at the events, circumstances, and people in our life correctly. What may seem to be bad may actually be good, and vice versa. I trust that even when things don't seem to be going my way, God is at work and will bring good out of it. This is a truth that Mary learned through her suffering. Mary is a model of virtue in many things, but foremost was her trust in God. That was evident right at the moment of the conception of Jesus when she accepted the role of mother of the Messiah even though she didn't understand the implications. She trusted, surrendered and said "Yes." (Luke 1:38)

Most of us have heard about president Abraham Lincoln and know he was a great president and man of God. Few, however, know about his road to the White House. Consider these facts about his life:

Failed in business in 1831
Defeated for legislature in 1832
Second failure in business in 1833
Suffers nevous breakdown in 1836
Defeated for speaker in 1838
Defeated for congress in 1843
Defeated for congress in 1848
Defeated for senate in 1855
Defeated for vice president in 1856
Defeated for senate in 1858
Elected President in 1860

It took 29 long years of failure, defeats and sufferings. Abraham Lincoln didn't give up! He was determined. He kept trying. He pressed on! Anyone who succeeds in life must deal with hardships. They aren't necessarily bad, but can provide the stuff of character.

One day the only survivor of a shipwreck was washed up on a small, uninhabited island. He prayed fervently for God to rescue him. Every day he scanned the horizon for help, but nothing seemed to be happening. Exhausted, he eventually managed to build a little hut out of dry driftwood to protect him from the elements and to store his few possessions.

Then one day, after scavenging for food, he arrived home to find his little hut in flames, the smoke billowing up to the sky. The worst had happened; everything was lost. He was stunned with grief and anger. "God, how could you do this to me?" he shouted.

A few hours later, he looked at the bay and there was a ship coming to shore. It had come to rescue him. "How did you know I was here?" asked the weary man. "We saw your smoke signal," they replied.

Even the so called "fires" in our lives can turn out to be good in God's providence.

DO NOT BE ANXIOUS
(Matthew 6:25)

I haven't always been sure about the leading and the providence of God in my life, but I trust. I'm not always sure about the people God surrounds me with, but I believe that it is for my good. I don't always know what God is doing, but I know deep within that God has a plan. What is good? What is bad? We need wisdom and insight to know truly. God makes all things work to good for those who love him; not some things, not a few things, *everything.*

Jesus taught, "The kingdom of heaven is like a merchant in search of fine pearls, who, on finding one pearl of great value, went and sold all that he had and bought it." (Matthew 13:45) It is interesting how pearls are formed. The oyster lives at the bottom of the sea somewhere and a piece of sand somehow gets into the opening in its shell. The sand will lodge inside the shell with the oyster. This irritates the oyster. Day after day the oyster will work on it and work on it. Finally, *in time*, the valuable pearl is produced.

Your irritations can be invitations to new life! Irritations can be irrigations of the Holy Spirit. Pearls are valuable and look beautiful. God desires the "pearls" of the Spirit. God wants you adorned with pearls of patience, rubies of righteousness, and gems of grace: these are valuable in God's eyes. You look beautiful in virtue. "Let not yours be the outward adorning with braiding of hair, decoration of gold, and wearing of fine clothing, but let it be the *hidden person of the heart* with the imperishable jewel of a gentle and quiet spirit, which *in God's sight is very precious.*" (1 Peter 3:3-4)

We all experience irritations every day. It could be a noisy or nosey neighbor. I have always been sensitive to noise. Barking dogs and leaf blowers upset me. Perhaps it is traffic you have to deal with. It could be a person you live with or an in-law. It seems to me that people in our life are like sandpaper.

When I used to work with my dad as a carpenter, we would work with sandpaper quite a bit. We would use it to smooth off rough edges on the wood. There were different grades of sandpaper to use depending on how rough the wood was. Some sandpaper was coarser than others. Some was very fine to do the final smoothing. God knows what your rough edges are and just what "grade" of people to use! Annoyances can be *announcements* of just what needs to change in you.

Speaking of "in-laws," did you know that our first Pope, St. Peter, was married? That's right. Mark 1:30-31 tells us the story. "Now Simon's (Peter's) mother-in-law lay sick with a fever, and immediately they told Jesus of her. And he came and took her by the hand and lifted her up, and the fever left her; and she served them." It was Archbishop Fulton Sheen who said, "Do you know why Peter denied Jesus three times? Because he healed his mother-in-law!"

Another one I heard was about a man who had his mother-in-law living with him and his wife for the last fifteen years of the mother-in-law's life. Finally, after fifteen long years with him, she died. He took her to the funeral home and the funeral director asked him a question. "Do you want to have her cremated or embalmed?" "Both," the man replied. "She's tricky!"

18
JOY IN PROGRESS
"How great our joy when we make a little progress walking the royal road of the cross!"
(St. Paul of the Cross)

JOYFUL, JOYFUL WE ADORE THEE

When I first began ministering, I was so serious. I mean after all, our faith is serious stuff and I am preaching about eternal life. However, over the years I met people whom I experienced as balanced theologically and funny. They began to show me that you can smile and laugh in church and it is okay. I began to loosen up and lighten up. Now, I tell jokes and have fun when I preach. I still maintain my seriousness, but humor is a way that I can proclaim the Gospel that relaxes me and most of my listeners. I have heard many comments from people that the humor appeals to them, and especially to their children.

Proverbs 17:22 states, "A cheerful heart is a good medicine, but a downcast spirit dries up the bones." Jesus' recipe for tribulations was laughter. "In the world you will have tribulation; but be of *good cheer*, I have overcome the world." (John 16:33) I have a couple of pictures of the laughing Jesus. One is in my Bible and the other on my dresser. In one of the pictures, Jesus' head is kicked back and all his teeth are showing as he laughs. Some bristle at this idea of Jesus, but Jesus was human! He laughed. God gave us the gift of laughter as a means of health and fun.

✝ Chapter 18 ✝

Cheerleaders cheer at sports games because when the going gets tough, the cheering helps the team and spectators through the hard moments. In the midst of the craziness of some of the situations we can get into, sometimes we just have to laugh. Suffering is sobering, but don't lose your sense of humor. It will help you through a lot of difficult situations. The person who laughs, lasts.

I saw a bumper sticker once that said, "If you are a Christian, inform your face." One of the most difficult things I had to get over as a preacher (and I still struggle with this at times) is people's faces. I go from place to place and, for the most part, I am not known in the various churches where I preach. I have to introduce myself and interest people in the mission I preach. I like to look into people's eyes when I speak. Sometimes I see the most glum looking faces. Doubt can enter my mind. I wonder, "Am I getting through to them?"

When I look out and see people smiling at me, they make such a difference! It encourages me. It helps me. It makes me feel like they are listening and know what I mean when I preach. Not many people shout "Amen!" in the Catholic church, but a smile is the next best thing.

I heard a story about a church service in Europe that was rather dull and boring. Present in the congregation was an enthusiastic charismatic Catholic. The priest's homily wasn't all that inspiring, but he did say some truthful things about Jesus. After each true statement the man in the pew would shout out "Amen!" Everyone turned around to look at him. As the priest continued to preach, suddenly he shouted out, "Yes, Alleluia!" Again, everyone turned to eye him.

Finally one of the ushers had had enough. He went over to the man and said to him, "Excuse me, we don't do that kind of thing in this church." "What do you mean?" replied the man, "I've got religion!" "You may have religion," said the usher in reply, "but you didn't get it here!"

What I find sad is that we can look so sour when we *should* be the happiest people on the face of the earth. To some we look like the sourest. How are we going to interest the world in our religion if it doesn't look like we are enjoying it ourselves? They are not going to want what we have. People are looking for joy and happiness. People not going to church aren't reading their Bibles, they are reading our faces.

Whenever I come into a parish to preach for the first time I am very aware that I am being observed. First impressions are important. People want to see if I've "got the goods." I think the number one area they are interested in is whether or not I am happy. Even though I may feel fearful or don't necessarily feel happy, I make the decision to try to smile. I don't want to be another sourpuss preacher up there. I want to be joyful and smile and make worship and hearing God's word a good experience. Samuel M. Shoemaker once said, "The surest mark of a Christian is not faith, or even love, but *joy*." I agree with that!

SAY CHEESE!

Mother Teresa was voted the number one most admired person of the twentieth century by a C.N.N. poll. She was called a "living saint" when she was alive because of her dedication to the poor and selfless service of love. She wrote a book called *One Heart Full of Love*. In this book she gives practical ideas about how to love. I'd like to quote one excerpt. "But I think if you look inside your own homes, you may notice how hard it is for you to smile at one another sometimes! And yet *smiling is the beginning of love*. Let's be willing to smile at one another. Yes, a smile is the beginning of love. And once we begin to love one another, the desire to do something more naturally follows."

I've always found that statement so simple, yet profound. A smile is the beginning of love. It is something all of us can do. She's not talking about running into burning buildings to save people. That's not the beginning of love, a simple everyday smile is. Try something for a moment. Right where you are, as you are reading this book, smile. Don't you feel better when you do? I find that my mood gets lifted when I get a "face lift" by smiling. Choosing to smile when you don't necessarily feel like it is loving and part of passionate living.

Last time I went to my dentist, I noticed some free cards he was handing out. This is what was on them.

A Smile

It costs nothing but creates much.
It enriches those who receive,
without impoverishing those who give.
It happens in a flash and
the memory of it sometimes lasts forever.
None are so rich that they can get along
without it, and none are so poor
but are richer for a smile.

> Yet it cannot be bought, begged,
> borrowed or stolen, for it is something
> that is no earthly good to anyone until
> it is given away.

I just had a new set of pictures taken to send in advance of my visit to parishes. They use these pictures for advertising purposes to try to attract people to the mission. Three different poses were taken of me. In all of them, I was smiling! I've noticed that whenever people get their pictures taken, they try to smile. That is because that is the way people want to be seen and remembered. You look best when you are smiling. Don't just smile for pictures, smile for people.

YOU CALL THIS PROVIDENCE?

It can be hard to laugh when you are dealing with hardships in your life. Even then, in spite of people, tribulations, circumstances or events in our lives, God makes all things work to good for those who love God. I've always thought the story of Joseph in the Old Testament illustrates this principle beautifully.

The story of Joseph can be found in the book of *Genesis*, chapters 37-50. I think one of the reasons the author spends 14 chapters of the first book of the Bible on Joseph is because this story teaches us such an important truth.

Remember Joseph was one of the twelve sons of Jacob (where we get the twelve tribes of Israel) who was the grandson of Abraham and the son of Isaac. Joseph was favored by his father and was given a long robe with sleeves. If that wasn't enough to incite his brothers' envy, Joseph was a dreamer and made the mistake of telling his brothers about his dream. Perhaps some of you have seen the play *Joseph and the Amazing Technicolor Dreamcoat*. That play tells the story of the life of Joseph.

The dream Joseph had was that one day all his brothers would bow down to him. The envy and anger of his brothers when he told them about his dream led them to throw him into a pit and sell him into slavery. (Now was this *bad* luck or *good* luck?) He was taken to Egypt. The Lord was with Joseph and God caused all that he did to prosper. (Genesis 39:3) His integrity was tested by his master's wife. She wanted him to commit adultery and because he wouldn't, she lied and had him thrown in prison. Sometimes when you do the right thing, wrong things seem to happen temporarily to test you.

The Lord was with Joseph in prison and showed him favor even there. (Genesis 39:21) No matter what prison you seem to be in, if God is with you, God will prosper you. It was in prison that God was doing a work in Joseph. Joseph had to learn trust, forgiveness and patience. It is crucial, if you are going to be used by God, that you be a person of integrity and virtue.

After *years* when it seemed he was forgotten, **suddenly**, Joseph was *brought hastily out* of the dungeon. (Genesis 41:14) That's exactly the way it is with God. One day you are in the pit, then suddenly you can get promoted to the palace. When God moves, things happen. Just because something doesn't seem to be happening today, keep trust, there is always tomorrow!

Joseph was promoted to be governor of all of Egypt, second only to the Pharaoh himself. Then, of course, came the fulfillment of his dream. His brothers, not recognizing who Joseph was, came and bowed before him with their faces to the ground. (Genesis 42:6) Now all the patience and forgiveness and integrity that Joseph learned from his "bad luck" showed in his actions. Instead of punishing his brothers for what they did to him, he revealed himself and said, "I am your brother Joseph whom you sold into Egypt." (Genesis 45:4)

Instead of being harsh and bitter, Joseph's beautiful comments displayed his trust and faith. "God sent me before you to preserve a remnant on earth, and to keep alive for you many survivors. So it was not you who sent me here, *but God*." (Genesis 45:7-8) Through all the time and pain and betrayal and danger Joseph experienced, he was able to see the hand of God leading and working in every situation.

Finally we read this wonderful statement illustrating what I have been writing about. "As for you, you meant evil against me; *but God meant it for good* . . ." (Genesis 50:20) What is this whole story of Joseph teaching us? God makes all things work to good for those who love him. Can you believe that right now God is at work in your situation? Can you sense that God is using the situation to purify you and bring you to integrity and promote you? Dare you trust that God is working to bring about good in your situation even though you can't see it now? A person who wants to live passionately must be a person of hope! As we read in Romans 5:3-4, "Suffering produces . . . hope, and hope does not disappoint us . . ." God can turn *your* tragedies into triumphs! You can cope through hope!

19
PURIFYING FIRE
"Cast yourself into the loving furnace of the Passion so that all the mold of your imperfections will be burned away. . . ."
(St. Paul of the Cross)

TRANSFORMED, NOT TRANSLATED!

During the Christmas season, on the Tuesday after Epiphany, our Church has a beautiful opening prayer. "Father, your Son became *like us* when he revealed himself in our nature: help us to become more *like him*." That is exactly what God is about in our lives. God is trying to make us like Jesus. An early church father spoke about Christmas this way, "God became man so that man could become God."

God is the potter and we are the clay. God's wonderful plan is revealed in Romans 8:29, "For those whom God foreknew he also predestined to be **conformed to the image of his Son**, in order that he might be the firstborn among many brothers and sisters." This is such a crucial verse in the Bible, because it reveals to us exactly what God is doing.

Many people come up to me and say, "Father, I go to church week after week and Sunday after Sunday. I pray and seek God, but I really don't know what God is doing in my life." Don't ever lose sight of Romans 8:29. Day after day, week after week, year after year its truth is at work. God is conforming us, reshaping us and transforming us into the image of Jesus!

Some think that they will be "transformed" here on earth in a moment, in the twinkling of an eye (1 Corinthians 15:52) But transformation is a *slow process of growth*. Like wine, we take time! Sometimes there can be a sudden spurt of growth, but in the long run, we need time.

FIRE-TRIED GOLD
(1 Peter 4:12)

Malachi 3:2-3 tells us that "he (Jesus) is like a refiner's fire and like fuller's soap; he will *sit* as a refiner and purifier of silver and he will purify the sons of Levi and refine them like gold and silver, till they present right offerings to the Lord." Refining takes time and needs the expertise of the refiner.

As you know, gold is purified and refined in the hot fire. I heard a story about a goldsmith. One day a married couple entered a store where there were all kinds of valuable gold and silver works. They enjoyed the work of this particular goldsmith so much that they wanted to meet him. The salesman took them to the back room of the store where the goldsmith was *sitting* looking intently into a pot. Beneath the pot was a blazing fire, and in the pot was molten gold.

The couple came over to him and introduced themselves. The goldsmith wouldn't remove his eyes from the pot. "What are you doing?" asked the couple. "I am purifying the gold," came the answer. "I must sit here and watch it closely. This is the crucial stage. If the fire gets too hot, the gold will be ruined. If there is not enough heat, it will cool with the impurities in it." "How do you know when the gold is ready?" queried the couple. "I know the gold is just right when I look into it and can see the reflection of my face," said the goldsmith.

God wants his face, his image, to shine through you and me. He knows precisely how much heat to give us and when: he sits as a refiner, the prophet Malachi tells us. God is active in the everyday situations of our life. God's great purpose is to make us like Christ.

When I say that God wants to make us Christ-like, that doesn't mean that he wants us to have long hair and a beard; rather, what God desires is that our hearts be regenerated to be like the sacred heart of Jesus. The sacred heart of Jesus is his heart of mercy, compassion, love, gentleness, humility and faith. We need "heart" transformation, a change of heart. God does "open heart" surgery. God comes into the lives of those open to him and surgically heals them. The writer of Psalm 51:10 pleads, "Create in me a clean heart, O God, and put a new and right spirit within me."

The psalmist prayed that because he knew what we all know, that deep within we fall short of the glory of God. There is sin. Selfishness runs wild. Carnality takes over. We don't love as we should. Jeremiah wrote, "The heart is deceitful above all things and desperately corrupt; who can understand it?" (Jeremiah 17:9) Paul lamented with frustration his own carnality, "I do not understand my own actions. For I do not do what I want, but I do the very thing I hate." (Romans 7:15) I have been a priest and a religious for many years now and I lament my sin. I want to do the right thing all the time, yet I fail. This grieves me deeply and keeps me in a state of brokenness and leaning on God. We are told that "a broken contrite heart God will not spurn." (Psalm 51:17) We must be broken to be put together.

We may not be perfect, but we are all being changed from glory to glory. Rest assured, as we allow God to work in us and cooperate with God, we are being changed. St. Paul talked about our reflecting the face of God. In order for this to happen, we must be changed into his likeness from one degree of glory to another by the Holy Spirit. (2 Corinthians 3:18) I'm in one degree of glory now, but I won't always stay there. There is an even more glorious future for us as we progress and go forward.

ALREADY, BUT NOT YET

Most of the time this is how we see growth: we move from point A to point B along a straight line of process and learning. Life is lived at some point along that line as we go forward. Sometimes we go back a bit. Sometimes we stay the same for a while, but hopefully, we are moving on and going forward toward the goal of being like Christ. Most of us are used to thinking of growth in these terms.

Paul the Apostle speaks of this linear process of growth many times in his writing. But, in addition, like a spiritual Einstein, Paul gives us a wonderful revelation of something even more profound. Paul speaks at times as if we are *already* something new and beautiful in Christ that we don't quite realize. 2 Corinthians 5:17 is the classic verse, "Therefore, if any one is in Christ, he is a new creation; the old has passed away, behold *the new has come.*" What Paul seems to be saying is that already we have within us the image of Christ brought to perfection. What has to happen is for us to *realize and accept* who we *already are* in Christ!

Paul made the profound and mystical statement that "It is no longer I who live, but Christ who lives in me."

(Galatians 2:20) Also, he taught, "But we *have* (now) the mind of Christ." (1 Corinthians 2:16) Paul had the mystical awareness that in some real sense he was *already whole* and renewed in and through the presence of Christ who lived within him.

Paul is telling us something profound: when we were baptized into the death and resurrection of Christ, we received the very life of Jesus and became a new creature. We are new *now*! We must now "put off" the old and "put on" the new. (Ephesians 4:24 and Colossians 3:10) I think Paul is telling us to realize and appreciate who we are *now* in Christ. You are new. The risen Jesus actually lives in you! Live like you are in Christ and Christ is in you. Instead of gradually becoming changed, know that you are changed now and live that way!

ON EAGLE'S WINGS

One story that illustrates this way of seeing ourself is the story about the eagle's egg that was taken out of its nest and put in with the chicken's eggs. After it hatched the eaglet grew up with the chickens, ate like a chicken, talked like a chicken, learned how to be a chicken and even thought he was a chicken. Every once in a while, he would see an eagle fly overhead and deep within, something stirred. In his heart of hearts, he dreamed and longed to fly and soar like an eagle, but as he looked around at everyone, he realized that he would always be just a chicken.

One day a great storm blew into the barnyard. The chickens were all blown aside, flapped their wings, and ran for cover in fear. The eagle, however, stood his ground. The gale winds forced the wings of the eagle open and he began to rise and fly. At first he was scared because he didn't think he could fly; after all, he was a chicken. Then he began to soar and *realized* that he was not a chicken at all, but he was truly a gracious eagle. It was the storm that awakened him to the truth of who he really was!

Perhaps you grew up in an abusive situation physically or emotionally. It could be that your parents told you that you were no good and would never amount to anything. Possibly your spouse doesn't understand you. Perhaps the people in your life are trying to squash your dreams and visions and are very negative about life. Although you live with these people, you don't have to be like them. Everything about God is positive. You have been restored deep inside through Christ! God will be your strength. You are beautiful inside and God wants to help you. Wait on God in trust and faith. "Those who wait for the Lord shall renew their strength, they shall mount up with wings like eagles, they shall run and not be weary, they shall walk and not faint." (Isaiah 40:31)

It's interesting that the U.S. postal service uses the image of an eagle as the symbol for their service. They chose the eagle symbol because eagles are majestic and beautiful in flight. Eagles soar. Eagles get it done. You are a new creation, an eagle, not a chicken.

YOU ARE GOD'S MASTERPIECE!

Another illustration may help you to understand. When I was in Rome, I saw many art works by Michelangelo, the great painter and sculptor of the sixteenth century. He did wonderful pieces of art like *Moses, David* and the *Pietà.* People marvel at his statues because they are so lifelike.

Once he was asked how he did it. How did he sculpt such works of art and create such masterpieces of beauty? Michelangelo, the man of faith, replied in a very unique way to this question. He said that when he came to the rock, he knew in his heart that God had *already* put the finished, perfect statue in there. All Michelangelo had to do was chip away the excess pieces!

That was St. Paul's vision too. God has already made us new. I love the way the Jerusalem Bible translates Ephesians 2:10, "We are *God's work of art*, created in Christ Jesus, to live the good life as from the beginning he had meant us to live it." You are God's work of art. You are his masterpiece.

God is like the master sculptor in our lives. He sees the potential, the possibility, the perfection and the beauty already in us. So what is God doing? God pulls out his holy hammer and purifying chisel and chips away the excess pieces. Maybe you have a "chip on your shoulder" that needs to be chipped away. Perhaps it is a cynical spirit that needs to be knocked off. Possibly it is a pattern of sin that God will work on. God sees who we are deep inside and is going to make sure we become that!

In addition, Ephesians 2:10 teaches that God *already prepared beforehand* the good works that he wants us to walk in. I believe that before the world began, God had a specific plan that was all laid out for me to become a priest of Jesus Christ. I had to discover and walk in this wonderful plan of God for my life. Few people actually realize how beautiful they are, and few walk in God's wonderful plan for their lives. I pray that you will awaken to your inner beauty and know that God has a good plan for you!

I know that seeing yourself as complete, new and whole *now* is a radical and new way of looking at yourself. However you envision the purification process, whether as a journey toward wholeness or as being complete in Christ now and needing some pieces chipped away, the truth of the matter is, we are all being transformed and changed. This takes place by a combination of God's activity and our cooperation. Metamorphosis is a marvelous and mysterious process.

BUTTERFLIES ARE FREE

I heard a story of a twelve-year-old boy who was studying insects in his science class around springtime. One day he was walking out in the forest and he looked up in a young tree and saw something. Right where a branch met the trunk of the tree the young man saw a cocoon.

The caterpillar crawls up the tree and spins a cocoon. In time and after a lot of work the cocoon is spun and hardens. Inside the cocoon, in secret, transformation takes place. No one sees it and no one knows about it. Through the genius of God's working, the caterpillar becomes a butterfly.

Deep within you, you are being changed. This book is changing you. Life is changing you. God is changing you. No one may see it and you may not even know it. But you are deeper than you think you are. You don't know everything there is to know about yourself. You are a mystery even to yourself. God is closer to you than you are to yourself. Trust that the process of change and transformation *is* at work in you, even if you don't feel it or seem to see any difference.

As the young boy looked up, he carefully grabbed hold of the cocoon and disconnected it from the tree and took it home with him. He put it on his desk and was observing it, knowing that something was going on. Just at that moment, a colorful yellow and black wing began to poke its way through the tiniest opening in the hardened cover. The cocoon shook back and forth as the wing pushed its way out more and more.

Finally after 20 minutes of this, the wing was half out, but the little boy had had enough. After all, how much patience does a young boy of twelve have? He went over to his mother's sewing kit and got a pair of scissors. He thought to himself, "I'll help that butterfly to get out." Meaning well, he carefully cut the hardened cocoon away from the wings so that the butterfly could come out and fly.

When the cocoon was fully cut away, the butterfly crawled out and tried to fly. All it could do was flip flop on the table. It couldn't fly. Its wings were misshapen and after a few minutes of flopping around, it finally stopped trying and lay over and died.

If you know anything about entomology (the study of insects) you will know that the butterfly actually needs to wrestle with the cocoon to force fluids out of the wing. Also, in the struggle, the blood flows to the wings. The fight makes the butterfly strong so that it can fly and be who it was meant to be. It's the fight that leads to flight!

The little boy, when he cut away the cocoon, thought he was helping the butterfly. In actuality he killed it!

Sometimes, in our spiritual immaturity, we pray like this: "Lord, please cut away my cocoon. If only I didn't have this illness in my life, then I would be happy. If only I didn't have this problem in my life, then I would be joyful. If only I had fewer trials, then . . ." God has a lot more wisdom and patience than a twelve-year-old boy with a pair of his mother's scissors. God knows we need the wrestling and the struggle and the fight with our cocoon so that we can fly and be who we were meant to be!

I love to watch butterflies. First of all, they are pretty. Their wings are colorful and lovely to look at. Each one is different. In addition, they go where they want. They fly, flit and flutter around and the world is their playground. Butterflies are free! They have suffered. They have been transformed. Because they have "gone through" their trial, they now enjoy the fulfillment of being who they are.

What God is deeply interested in is our inner transformation and metamorphosis. Whatever cocoon you may have in your life at this moment is *exactly what you need* so that you can fly spiritually and be who you were meant to be in Christ. We are being purified. Our selfishness is dying. God isn't so much interested in your having a comfortable life as in your being conformed to the image of Jesus Christ.

It is very important that you understand this as **the** major work of God in your life. Everything you experience for the rest of your life will be geared toward making you whole and holy in Christ. One of the earliest written prayers in the New Testament comes from Paul's letter to the Thessalonians and speaks of sanctification. "May the God of peace himself *sanctify you wholly*; and may your spirit and soul and body *be kept sound and blameless* at the coming of our Lord Jesus Christ. He who calls you is faithful, and he will do it." (1 Thessalonians 5:23-24) This was Paul's prayer for the early Christians at Thessalonica and for us.

ACCEPTANCE IS THE ANSWER

As I mentioned in my section on compassion, the twelve step program is an effective way for people who suffer to help other people. People in the twelve steps always pray a prayer that I really like. This prayer, attributed to Reinhold Niebuhr, has appealed to me for years and makes a lot of sense. I'd like to offer it for all of you reading this book.

Serenity Prayer

God, grant me the Serenity
to accept the things I cannot change,
Courage to change the things I can,
and the Wisdom to know the difference.

We are all searching for serenity and peace in our lives. We may not always get everything the way we want it, but some things we simply have to accept and "let be" just the way they are. I live with eight people in community and every one of them is different. I have found that if I want serenity, I have to stop trying to change them to be who I want them to be and accept them for who they are. I am also learning to accept myself as I am. This leads to inner peace.

I was preaching in Los Angeles about the serenity prayer when a woman gave me this reflection about acceptance.

Acceptance

Acceptance is the answer to all my problems today. When I am disturbed, it is because I find some person, place, thing, or situation — some fact of my life unacceptable to me. I can find no serenity until I accept that person, place, thing, or situation as being exactly the way it is supposed to be at this moment. Nothing, absolutely nothing, happens in God's world by mistake; unless I accept life completely on life's terms, I cannot be happy. I need to concentrate on what needs to be changed in me and in my attitudes.

In addition to acceptance, the serenity prayer asks for "the courage to change the things we can." The common notion seems to be that we can't change things. I believe that some situations are changeable. We must work for peace and strive to forgive. That takes courage. I am a preacher as well as a priest. I believe that the words I speak **do** change people, otherwise I wouldn't be preaching. I believe that the words of this book will help you to change.

There are parts of ourselves that we can change. We are responsible for this, but there are major parts of us that only God can transform. In addition, you do have an effect on your children and on your spouse. It takes tremendous courage and love to try to effect change. I try to take responsibility for myself *and others*. We are our brother's and sister's keeper. (Genesis 4:9)

We must learn from our mistakes and our experiences. This is one of the hallmarks of wisdom. One definition for wisdom is "learned experiences that guide us to prosper in the future." I remember when I first came to Christ, I used to share Jesus a bit too strongly with people one on one. I learned what worked and what didn't work. I learned from my experience. Now I'm better at accepting situations and people that I cannot change. Yet, I still look for the courage to change the situations and people that I can, including myself. This has been a book about learning. Let life teach you and listen well! I pray you learn the wisdom to know the difference between what you can and cannot change in yourself and others.

20
CLOTHED WITH CHRIST
"... Be completely clothed with the most pure faith and love for Jesus Christ."
(St. Paul of the Cross)

JESUS CHRIST THE SAME YESTERDAY, TODAY AND FOREVER (Hebrews 13:8)

One part of the Eucharistic prayer that really touches me each time I pray it comes from Eucharistic Prayer II during the "institution narrative." Immediately after we pray for the Holy Spirit to make the gifts of bread and wine holy, I pray these words, "Before he was given up to death, a death he *freely accepted* . . ." Jesus accepted his Passion. He answered the call and made good choices. Philippians 2:5 tells us to "Let this same attitude and mind be in you which was in Christ Jesus."

Jesus was a man of beautiful character and grace. He had serenity. He is the noble and royal Prince of Peace. He accepted life and even his own death in a marvelous way. No matter the struggle, he didn't deny it or run from it in cowardice. He faced it and embraced it. Jesus courageously spoke out against injustice and changed people because of his attitude. Jesus learned from life and grew and developed in wisdom before God and people. He treasured life and lived passionately.

Jesus paved the way for us. Hebrews 12:1-2 tells us to "run with perseverance the race that is set before us, *looking to Jesus* the pioneer and perfecter of our faith, who for the joy that was set before him endured the cross . . ."

A pioneer is a trailblazer who ventures into the unknown. Jesus has blazed a trail for us. We have a way we can follow. He is the way to passionate living. He will help us to have a selfless positive attitude. He is already victorious.

The idea of "perfecter" of our faith has to do with making complete and bringing us to maturity. In order to come to maturity in the spiritual life, we must keep our eyes *fixed on Jesus*. We must live our lives centered in Jesus Christ.

I am writing this book during the Jubilee Year (2000) in our Church. Many churches have a banner hung up with a circle on it. Within the circle are the words, "Christ, yesterday, today and forever." This comes from Hebrews 13:8, "Jesus Christ is the same yesterday and today and forever." Jesus doesn't change or fade or pass away. He is consistent, balanced, stable and the key to passionate living. Look to him and build your life on the foundation that is Christ.

This excerpt of prose is attributed to St. Patrick and is called "St. Patrick's Breastplate."

> Christ be with me,
> Christ before me,
> Christ behind me,
> Christ in me,
> Christ beneath me,
> Christ above me,
> Christ on my right,
> Christ on my left,
> Christ where I lie,
> Christ where I sit,
> Christ where I arise.

HERE I AM LORD! SEND ME
(Isaiah 6:8)

When I was professed in the Passionist community, it was the custom to take a title along with our profession. I have always had a sense of wonder whenever I heard the story of Jesus in the garden of Gethsemane. I am amazed at his selfless attitude. When I professed my vows as a Passionist, I took the name Cedric of Jesus in Gethsemane. One of the reasons I took that name is because I wanted my "Yes" to be united to the wonderful "Yes" of Jesus in the garden of Gethsemane. He could have run and hidden, but he humbly submitted to God's will for his life and said, "Yes, your will be done."

Sometimes when we pray the Our Father, we can rattle off the prayer so quickly that we don't even think of what we are saying. What we are truly asking for, however, is for *God's* will to be done, not *ours*. In the sacramentary, the second option for introducing that prayer talks about the "courage" to pray the Our Father. It takes courage to ask for God's will to be done. It takes daring to say "Yes" to God.

YES AND AMEN!
(2 Corinthians 1:20)

When I was preaching in San Antonio some years back, a young man gave me a framed poster. It is a beautiful portrait of one hole on a golf course with the orangey glow of the sun rising behind it. Underneath the picture in large letters is the word PASSION. This quote is beneath it: "There are many things in life that will catch your eye, but only a few that will catch your heart. . . . Pursue those."

I believe that Jesus has "caught" your heart. He lived an extraordinarily passionate life. Pursue him with passion.

God's great plan is for us to be Christ-like. We have been saved by his Cross, now we must be sanctified, purified and brought to maturity. This is a process that will take the rest of our lives. Jesus lived his life passionately and came to bring us his abundant life. As you keep your eyes fixed on Jesus and live through him, with him, and in him, I pray that you will grow and continue to say "Yes" to God with your life. Your continuous "Yes" in every circumstance will lead you to live passionately!

Dag Hammarskjold, the former Secretary General of the United Nations, penned a prayer in his book *Markings* that has always touched me. I leave it as my prayer for you.

"For all that has been–Thanks.
For all that will be, YES!"

ABOUT THE AUTHOR

Fr. Cedric Pisegna, C.P. is a Passionist priest who professed vows in September 1985. He was born in Springfield, Massachusetts and graduated from the University of Massachusetts at Amherst with B.S. in Social Work and a minor in Business. In addition, he has studied Philosophy at Southern Illinois University and has studied Speech and Drama at Northwestern University in Chicago. Fr. Cedric graduated from the Catholic Theological Union at Chicago in May 1990, receiving his Master of Divinity degree with Bible Specialization. He was ordained a priest on June 29, 1991.

Presently, Fr. Cedric preaches retreats and missions throughout the United States and Canada, ministering out of the Passionist retreat complex in Houston, Texas. He has preached over 300 missions for some 20 years. Fr. Cedric produces a program for TV & Radio, *Live with Passion!*, which presently airs in numerous cities. He has a number of CDs and DVDs on Christian living. In addition he has authored 15 books.

If you would like to share a testimony, help received from this book, or to schedule a mission in your parish, contact Fr. Cedric at:

Fr. Cedric Pisegna, C.P.
430 Bunker Hill Rd.
Houston, TX 77024

E-Mail: frcedric@frcedric.org
Website: www.frcedric.org

INSPIRATIONAL TEACHINGS BY FR. CEDRIC PISEGNA, C.P.

Books:
1. Live Passionately!
2. Glorious Holy Spirit
3. Thy Kingdom Come!
4. You Can Change
5. Death: The Final Surrender
6. Come Encounter Jesus
7. Golf & God
8. Eucharist: A Living Sacrifice
9. God's Not Boring!
10. A Retreat with Fr. Cedric
11. He Touched Me
12. You Can Be Happy: A Lifestyle of Well-Being
13. Kept in Christ
14. Seasons of Life
15. The Sacred Walk

Additional Inspirational Teaching Sets:
Fr. Cedric has produced hundreds of CD's and DVD's that will deepen your relationship with God and inspire you to Live with Passion!

To place an order online or for a complete listing of Fr. Cedric's teachings visit
www.frcedric.org

For ordering by mail contact:
JC Productions • Jim & Janice Carleton
2931 N. Willamette Blvd.
Portland, OR 97217 • (503) 289-1942
E-mail:Jim@frcedric.org • Website:www.frcedric.org

THE CONGREGATION OF THE PASSION

The Passionists are a religious community in the Catholic Church. They were founded in 1741 in Italy. The founder of the Passionists was Paul Daneo (St. Paul of the Cross). Their headquarters is in Rome, Italy. They are in 56 countries around the world. The major ministry of the Passionist priests, brothers and sisters is prayer and evangelization.

A Passionist religious professes vows of poverty, chastity, and obedience. Along with these is the unique first vow of a Passionist: to remember and meditate upon the Passion of Jesus and to proclaim its meaning to the world. The sign that Passionists wear on their religious habit (Jesu XPI Passio) means "The Passion of Jesus Christ." A familiar saying of Passionists is: "May the Passion of our Lord be ever in our hearts."

For more information about the Passionists or if you are interested in a religious vocation, please contact:

Vocation Director
Passionist Community
5700 N. Harlem Ave.
Chicago, IL 60631
773-631-6336

Websites:
www.passionist.org
www.frcedric.org

It is my intent to give credit for use of copyrighted material contained in this book. If such credit has inadvertently been omitted, please contact me at frcedric@frcedric.org so subsequent printings will contain the appropriate acknowledgment.